JOURNEY IN PRAYER

SEVEN DAYS OF PRAYER WITH JESUS

John. F. Smed

with Justine Hwang

and Leah Yin

Published by Prayer Current
106 – 1033 Haro Street
Vancouver, BC V6E 1C8
CANADA

Study Questions & Appendices: Justine Hwang
Cover Design, Illustrations & Book Layout: Leah Yin Studio
Map Grid: Erick Villagomez

WWW.PRAYERCURRENT.COM

DEDICATED

To Edith Schaeffer & Donald Drew
who set me on this road,
To Archie Parrish who kept me at it,
To Justine who helps cut new trails,
Especially to Caron,
who walks this path with me.

Introduction

Prayer is not everything, but everything is by prayer.

Ray Ortlund

Every believer desires to pray. Prayer is evidence of God's Spirit within us. It is our birth cry. Prayer is as important to our soul as breath is for our body. Yet we often struggle to pray. Sometimes we pray only a few minutes a day. Other times not at all. We want to pray with passion, yet many of our prayers are tedious and boring. We want to change our world through prayer, yet much prayer seems one way. It bounces back "return to sender."

To be a Christian without prayer is no more possible than to be alive without breathing.
MARTIN LUTHER

How can we move through this inertia to achieve vital and effective prayer? Apparently, just "saying our prayers" is not enough. Vital prayer requires a compelling purpose. We need to know the "why" of prayer. Effective prayer requires direction. We need to know the "how" of prayer. Jesus offers help. With him "we have a prayer." He gives us a simple but purpose-filled pattern to follow. We know it as the Lord's Prayer. He spoke it like this:

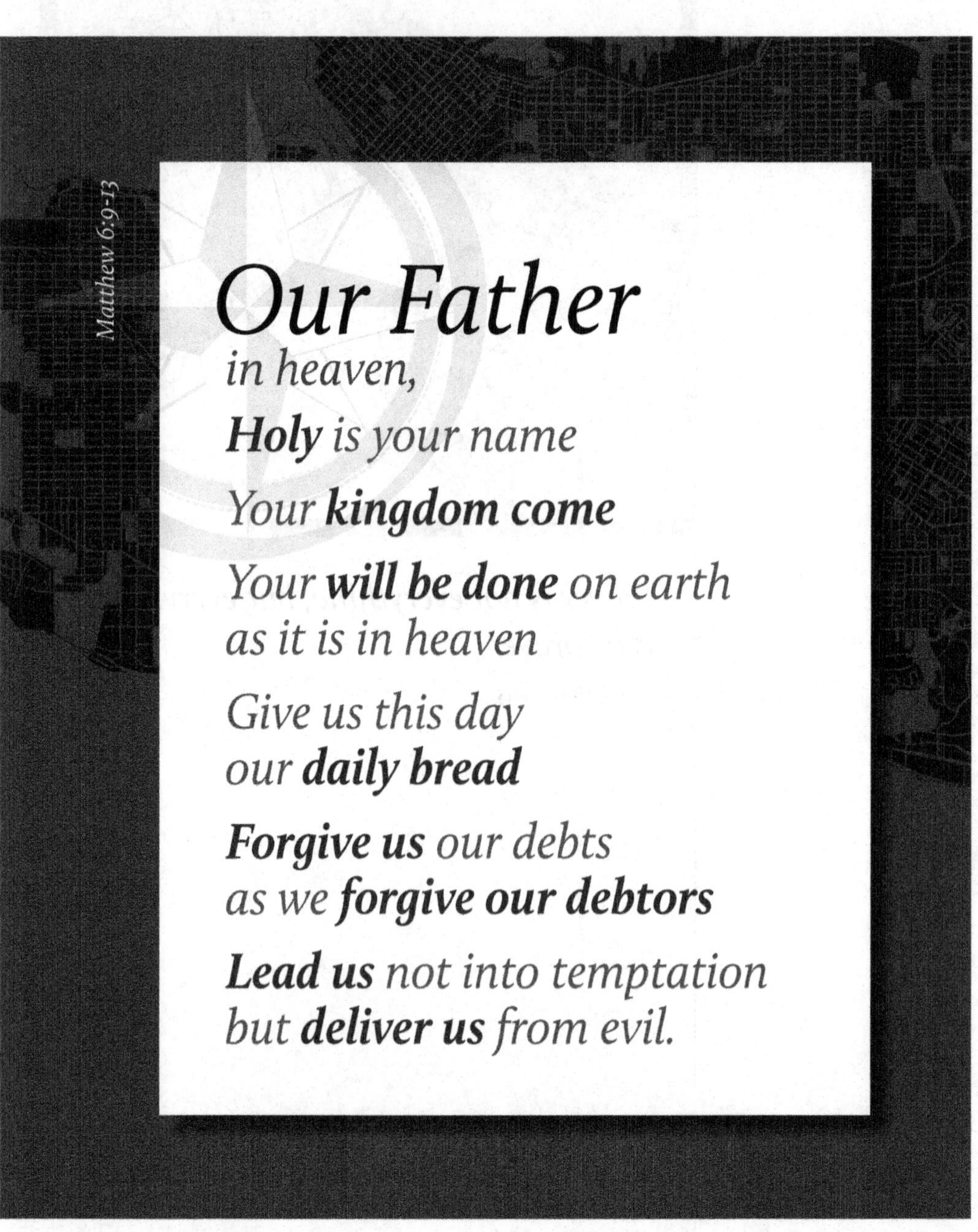

This is Jesus' prayer. It is how he prayed as he lived and loved among us. It is how he taught his disciples to pray. This prayer is filled with Jesus. It contains his agenda and his strategy for his present and coming kingdom. The secret to growing in faith and the key to reaching the world are found in its seven petitions.

Jesus is God's only Son. By faith we also become sons and daughters of our Father in heaven:

> *Because you are sons God has sent the Spirit of his Son into our hearts crying out, 'Abba' Father!*

Galatians 4:6

God always answers the prayer of his Son. He will always hear the prayers of his adopted sons and daughters as they pray it too.

Because this prayer is filled with Jesus, it is filled with purpose. Because this prayer is certain to be answered, it is filled with power. Jesus wants us to pray it faithfully. He invites us to pray it personally. He calls us to pray it in community.

This study, with application questions, is designed for personal and for group study. I have found the pattern and purpose of a well-ordered but simple prayer list sequence to be the best way to make Jesus' prayer my prayer. Throughout this book we will present this prayer in a seven section format - one day at a time, and one petition for each day. The outcome will be a seven day structure - a prayer list sequence for use in personal daily prayer.

Using Jesus' prayer as an outline for our prayers is not a new idea. Since he spoke it, millions of believers have used it as a guideline. Using a prayer list for more than thirty years, I adapted my prayers to this structure several years ago. As a congregation, Grace Vancouver has also been using Jesus' prayer as a format.

Prayer is the root, the fountain, the mother of a thousand blessings.
CHRYSOSTOM

From personal and church experience, I know praying with purpose makes a difference. As we study and practice Jesus' prayer, good things happen. We experience answers to prayer. Our prayer life gains momentum and spontaneity. A passion for God awakens. Awareness of the supernatural dimension of life becomes acute. Hope for our city is renewed. We find new boldness to step up to God, and courage to step out and help others. We experience the reality that God hears and answers prayer.

It is my hope and desire to encourage you in your prayer life. I hope this reflection will be helpful. If it is, all thanks goes to the One who gave us this prayer.

John F. Smed
Grace Vancouver Church

Prayerful Pondering

Questions for Reflection

Feel free to use the pages of this book as a travel log of sorts. Highlight what resonates with you or challenges you. Write your own questions. Record key discoveries. Explore your thoughts by doodling or scribbling your prayers, meditations, emotions, epiphanies, enigmas – whatever God brings to you.

Most important, let Jesus guide you; he will show you the Father's heart.

* What are the reasons you desire to pray?

To have a close relationship with my Lord
To ask Him to work and then experience His supernataral intervention

* What are your struggles with prayer?

Distractions, time, mind wandering

* What has been your experience with the Lord's prayer, if any?

I love the Lord's prayer!

* What are you hoping for your prayer journey as you delve into this book?

Jesus to meet with me

Summary of Key Idea(s) *What key thought(s) do you want to remember or revisit?*

Personal Prayer Response

Write a letter to God and write your struggles, desires and hopes for the journey ahead.

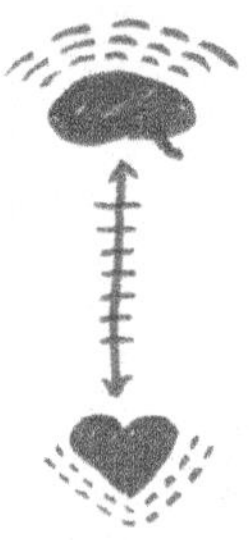

Prayer Practice

Prayer translates our thoughts (or what we think we understand) into a deeper reality. Prayer helps translate our head knowledge into heart experience of God's love.

Plan to take some time at the end of each chapter to practice prayer, using thoughts ignited by "Prayerful Pondering" questions, "Prayer Prompts" and "Prayer Patterns" to guide your prayers.

Try writing out your prayers as a record of your communication and growing relationship with God. By the end of this study, you may be encouraged to recognize God in new ways as you pray his priorities into your heart and life.

Our Father In Heaven

DAY **1** 2 3 4 5 6 7

In giving us these words 'Our Father,'
God binds himself to us.
LUTHER

This is the nature of the encounter,
not that I am stumbling toward
the Abba Father, but that Abba Father
is coming towards me.
STEPHEN VERNEY

DAY I

Our Father In Heaven

Today's Priority

* As we come to know and trust our heavenly Father, we turn from our orphan aloneness. We increasingly immerse ourselves in his eternal "Daddyness."

Purpose and Outcome of this Prayer

* We enjoy freedom from fear of rejection and punishment in all its forms. Our Father gifts us with his acceptance. We do not need to prove our worthiness.

Prayer is not one-way. It is two-way.
Prayer is not only about us getting through to God – so he can understand us and our needs. Prayer is about God getting through to us – so that we can know him and discover his fatherly love for us. When we pray, "Our father," we are asking that we might come to know him better. We ask that we might enjoy and rest in our royal adoption as God's children which we are granted because of our faith relationship with Jesus.

Matthew 6:7

According to Jesus, our prayers fail if they are just one way. Jesus says, "When you pray, do not keep babbling like pagans." Ritual incantations, relentless repetition and long explanations are indications of "one-way" prayer. When Tibetan Monks spin a prayer wheel, or someone endlessly recites the rosary, they are involved in "one-way" prayer. Luther said, "Few words and much meaning is Christian prayer. Many words and little meaning is pagan prayer."

The prayer Jesus teaches us is two-way. In two-way communication we look for a reply when we speak. In two-way prayer the father's reply confirms and cements his bond with his child. This kind of intimate and personal prayer is part of our father-child relationship with God. We come to realize that God is eager to know and enjoy us – even more than we desire to know and enjoy him.

As we grow in our comprehension of who God is, in our deepening understanding of him as our Father, we begin to have comfort, freedom and confidence in talking with him. We gain assurance in this Father-child relationship. We feel confident that we are heard by him, and that he will answer and give us what we need.

We are adopted – chosen – by our heavenly Father

God's eager love for us is expressed in the redemptive concept of adoption. Recently I had a conversation with a friend which reminded me of this.

Stan and Lori made several trips to Russia to adopt a little boy named Nicholas. Each trip they spent time with him but were not allowed to take him home. Each time they left the orphanage, it was heart-rending to leave him behind.

By the time I met Nicholas he was a beautiful little boy, full of life with curly auburn hair. Stan told me about his prior condition. The situation in his orphanage was desperate. Nicholas was covered in sores and was in ill health because of unsanitary conditions. He was seldom held.

I said, "Wow. With you and Lori, Nicholas just won the lottery of adoption."

Without a blink, Stan replied, "No John. You're wrong. We are the lucky ones. We won the lottery here. No one in the world could be happier than we are to have Nicholas as our son."

His words struck me. It made me think about my "sonship" with God. I asked Stan, "I wonder, do you think that God is just as happy to have us as his children? As well as thinking how great it is for us to be his children, is it possible that God is the one who is thrilled about being our adopting Father?"

The name "father" gets God's attention

Jesus opens the doors to heaven when he permits us to address God as our Father. God obliges himself to us in this name. It is when we use the name "father" that we get his attention.

My children are the only ones who use "Dad" when addressing me. It is their exclusive privilege. In fact Dad is the only name they use when they talk to me. My kids do not call me anything but Dad.

If one of my children calls me "mister" they probably won't get my attention. If they want my attention they call me "Dad." If I am not watching a hockey game, this name gets through to me every time.

It is the same with God. We can try praying to a "Higher Power," we can meditate on the "Ground of Being," we can study the "Inner light" or acknowledge a "Divine Spirit." I doubt we will command God's attention with generic phrases like this. We get God's full attention when we call him by his favorite name – "Father."

In the same way, when Jesus prays to God he calls Him "Father." Although there are 72 names for God in the Old Testament, and several more in the New Testament, every time Jesus addresses God, he calls him "Father."

"Father, I thank you that you hear me always."

"Father, I thank you that you have hidden these things from the wise and revealed them to the children."

"Father, protect them by the power of your name, the name you gave me, that they may be one as we are one."

Gospel of John & Luke

"Father, I want those you have given me to be with me where I am, and to share my glory."

"Father, glorify me with the glory I had with you before the world began."

"Father, if it be your will take this cup from me."

"Father, forgive them, for they know not what they do."

Only the Son of God has a natural right to use the name "Father."
In his very nature Jesus is the "only begotten Son of the Father."

Heavenly adoption made possible

If calling God "Father" is the exclusive right of Jesus the Son of God, how did we come to have this incredible privilege?

Simply this, when we trust in Jesus for forgiveness and eternal life, he confers upon us his own Royal Sonship status. By adoption, we become a true son or daughter of God. We are sons and daughters in Jesus' Sonship! This means God views us not only as his children. He views us the same as his only Son – along with all the benefits and access to him that Jesus has. This should take our breath away. This is the key to all effective prayer.

In his letter to the Galatian Christians the apostle Paul explains the truth of our adoption through faith in Jesus in dramatic terms:

Galatians 4:4-7

But when the time had fully come, God sent his son, born of a woman, born under law, to redeem those under the law, that we might receive the full rights of sons. Because you are sons, God sent the Spirit of his Son into our hearts, the Spirit who calls out, "Abba, Father." So you are no longer a slave but a son; and since you are a son, God has made you also an heir.

In prayer we now call him "Abba" – an affectionate term a Jewish child uses to call his Father. "Abba" means "daddy." This has enormous consequences in our relationship with God. As sons and daughters we are set free from slavish need to gain God's acceptance by our own self-righteousness and works. We are given the very Spirit of Jesus, the only Son of the Father to live within us. Now we are able to leave behind our orphan aloneness and rest in the eternal "Daddyness" of our God.

What this looks like when it comes to prayer

When you become a child of God you are able to come to God in freedom. You are freed from the relentless demands of the law, from the guilt and penalty of sin. You no longer have to plead your good works to earn your way to God. Once you have trusted in Christ, you are God's child and nothing can ever take this from you. It is final, complete and unconditional. Each time you pray, you can assume your sonship position with God. As the writer of the book of Hebrews writes,

Hebrews 4:16

Let us then approach the throne of grace with confidence, so that we may receive mercy and find grace to help us in our time of need.

When you talk to God, you no longer have to do penance and beat yourself up for your sins. You are forgiven the second you confess. Because of his love for you, his costly love in Jesus, he bears no grudge and remembers no sin. He removed the guilt and punishment of the law the day he allowed his Son to be your substitute on the cross.

Maybe you are religious. You are earnestly seeking the truth. But you are looking for something more than religion. You want more than trying to live a good life. You want more than a church service. Well, this is the "more"! Becoming a son or daughter of God is the real thing. Jesus invites you into a personal relationship with God where you can address him in an intimate way – as his very own child. You can call him "Daddy." You can leave behind the trappings of religion and put on the full joy of being his child.

Watch any child take their rightful place with their parent. I think of our own grand daughter Kaiya. When she comes into our home, she doesn't sit in a corner hiding, waiting for us to notice her. She just takes over. Without saying a word, she says, "I am here." When Kaiya comes to our house, we don't need TV or videos. She is all the entertainment we need. She leaves no time or attention left over for anything or anyone else! She runs up to her grandmother and simply demands her attention. She makes no apologies and shows no regrets. This is her right. This is her privilege as our grand daughter. All she has to say is "Papa" and my heart melts. She can ask for anything she wants. I might say no sometimes, but I could never be offended, no matter what she asks.

When I pray "Our Father" I know I experience the results of this sonship. I get to surrender my self-ownership. I gladly let go of my fierce self-determination. I get to leave that orphan aloneness I always feel within myself. I learn to immerse myself in the eternal Daddyness of God. I just receive and rest in the presence of God – where I belong. I know that I can demand his attention. He will never be too busy. I can ask him for anything I need. He will never be offended. He is willing to listen. He is able to answer.

He is our Father "in heaven"

Heaven is a place that is filled with God, teeming with his splendid glory and pregnant with joy and worship. While on earth, Jesus could not wait to return to heaven,

> *And now, Father, glorify me in your presence with the glory I had with you before the world began.* *John 17:5*

When Jesus says we should pray to "our Father in heaven" he encourages us to come before him with great confidence and assurance – like children coming to a loving father. Dwelling in the eternal reality of heaven, God is the original perfect and changeless Father – "from whom all fatherhood derives." *Ephesians 3:15*

There are many weak and neglectful fathers in the world. Even loving parents can fail you. Your Father in heaven will never fail you. He will never abuse, neglect or use you. His love for you will never corrupt or diminish.

Your status as a son or daughter is as certain and eternal as his Fatherhood. You need never feel like an orphan again. When you pray to him as "Father" he will always hear and answer you. He longs to hear you pray. His eye is upon you, and "His ears are open to [your] cry." *Psalm 34:15*

Note that "Our Father" is the first request of this prayer

Jesus wants us to start our prayer in the Spirit of his Sonship. If it were up to us, we might pray differently. We might want to jump right into prayers of confession – just to get rid of a bad conscience. We might start by crying out, "Help Lord! I am drowning here. I need you now!" But Jesus teaches something different, something essential about prayer here. We are to begin our prayer by bonding with God as Father.

In prayer we wage a mighty warfare. In prayer we wrestle against the anxiety and unworthiness we feel within us.
LUTHER

It is not helpful to run through the Lord's Prayer as a series of unrelated requests. If we start solidly with "Our Father," the rest of our prayer will be transformed. When we come to him in the experience and expectation of a child of God, each part of Jesus' prayer will be a Father-child dialogue.

For example, when we pray "Hallowed be your name," we pray for our father's name to be held in honor. What child is not jealous for his father's honor? Unless something is terribly wrong between a parent and child, no child can sit idly by when his father's name is dragged through the mud. If every child defends their earthly father, how much more should children of a heavenly Father jealously defend their Father's name? God's children are grieved when his name is cursed or mocked, and saddened when people misunderstand his justice and goodness. We are eager that men, women, and children should come to know and enjoy him as Father too. All this is included in "Hallowed be your name." All this is intimately connected to "Our father, who is in heaven."

As we pray each request of Jesus' prayer, we keep in mind that we are coming before a kind and generous Father, who is willing and able to hear and answer us. We ask boldly, because we know he is not offended. Teresa of Avila said, "You pay God a compliment when you ask great things of him." Jesus said, like every good father, your Father in heaven "delights to give good gifts to his children."

Matthew 7:11

Confident and effective prayer begins with "Our Father." We start here. We can go no further until we know him as Father. This precious truth should be carried into all our requests.

Conclusion

Remember Nicholas?

Stan and Lori went to Russia one last time to finish the adoption procedure. They had to sign the papers, pay all the fees, and then they could finally take him home. At this point Stan steps into the room and sees Nicholas in his orphan environment. He is covered in "scabies" – a bright red rash caused by small parasites. He has blisters on the bottom of his feet, the palms of his hands, and all over the inside of his mouth. This "hand, foot, and mouth" disease is common in unsanitary conditions like this orphanage. He reeks. The orphanage does not have money for diapers so he is often left in his own excrement. With his voice breaking, Stan tells me, "I could see him. I looked at him in all his distress. I just wanted to hold him. I wanted to comfort and heal him. But more than anything else, I wanted Nicholas to know just how much Lori and I love him."

What a beautiful picture of God's adoption of us. He sees us in the orphanage of the world. With a breaking heart, he notices the "scabies" of our discontent, the blisters of our unhappiness, yes, the stench of the sin we have too long remained in.

What does he do? Does he reject, despise and judge us – as we might be afraid he would? No. He does not. He does the exact opposite. He embraces us. He heals, cleans, and forgives us in his grace. Now he speaks tender and gracious words of love and mercy to us; he adopts us to be his sons and daughters. He pays all the costs of our adoption in the sacrifice of Jesus. Now he takes us home to live with him forever. Now we call him "Daddy."

DAY I

Prayerful Pondering

Questions for Reflection

* How might prayer be different by addressing God generically as a "higher power" in contrast to calling him specifically "Father"?

* How does an orphan's prayer differ from a son or daughter's prayer?

* How much are your prayers about asking for God's help in contrast to bonding with God as Father? How would starting with "God as Father" influence your prayers?

Summary of Key Idea(s)

What key thought(s) do you want to remember or revisit?

Prayer Prompts: *Use these points to guide your prayers. Try writing out your prayers.*

When we pray "Our Father in heaven":

* We thank God for his Fatherhood. We thank him for choosing us and adopting us into his family. We enjoy and soak in his "Daddyness."

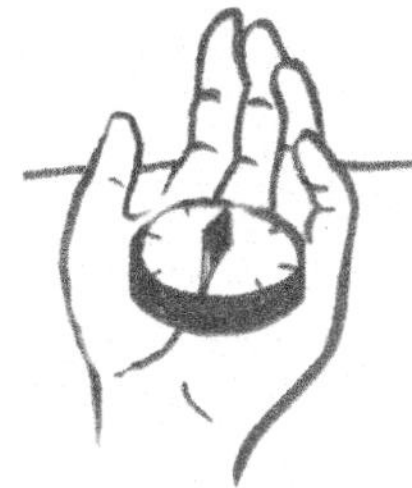

Creative Prayer Exploration

Prayer is conversation with God. We hear from God through his Word, the Bible, through thoughts or images he plants in our minds or hearts. Like all conversations, prayer is not linear; it's organic, growing in multiple directions like a tree's branches and roots simultaneously expanding.

Use words, images, color, and space to depict ideas and connections between various themes. You don't need to be an artist or have drawing skill; simply be open, have fun and see how God may use your scribblings to reveal insights you might not otherwise see.

DAY I

Prayer Practice:
Preparing for a Daily Pattern for Prayer

Overview

Throughout this book, we will lead you through a pattern and sequence for prayer that focuses on one priority from Jesus' prayer each day. Today you will apply the pattern to "Our Father in heaven."

Pattern for Prayer ► *Applied to "Our Father in heaven"*

1 *Priority & Promise*

Praise God for his promises & priorities

Start by focusing on the priority **UPWARD to God.** Allow the Holy Spirit to guide you through the priority for the day.

Praise Jesus for the priority. Meditate on **what it means,** what it reveals about God, about Jesus' passion and purpose.

* *Ponder the Father's love for you and delight in you. Meditate on the Father-child relationship that is yours in Christ.*

2 *Passions*

Pray God's promises & priorities into **your own heart**

Next pray the priority **INWARD into your heart.** Talk with God about your present heart state, allowing him to thoroughly examine and encourage you.

Ask Jesus to **transform your heart** and life to be more like his.

* *Thank him for growth you see in how you are receiving his love. Confess where you struggle to believe, and desire more of his love.*
* *Ask God to give you a child's joy, release from fear, and unbelief. Ask for his love to be stronger than your own struggles.*

3 *People*

Pray God's promises as a **blessing to others**

Now pray **OUTWARD for others to experience more of God**'s promises.

Pray for **people,** your loved ones, other individuals, ministries, your church, city, and the world.

* *Pray for specific people you know who struggle with accepting God's love. Pray for them to come to know God as Father.*
* *Pray for the prayer life of your church to be rich.*

4 *Praise*

Praise God for all his blessings

End by **praising God** for his blessings and answers to prayer.

Recall how God has been present. Remember to **thank** him.

* *Praise God for being our Father. Thank him for answers, blessings, or insights he reveals to you in your prayers.*

Personal Pattern for Prayer

Your prayer life will grow in depth, direction, passion and purpose by praying through one priority of Jesus' prayer each day using this sequence. Use Jesus' prayer as a framework to map your prayer. A further guide to this prayer pattern begins on page 107.

Personal Prayer Response

1 Priority & Promise

Praise God for his promises and priorities

2 Passions

Pray God's promises & priorities into your own heart

3 People

Pray God's promises as a blessing to others

4 Praise

Praise God for all his blessings

Holy Is Your Name

DAY 1 **2** 3 4 5 6 7

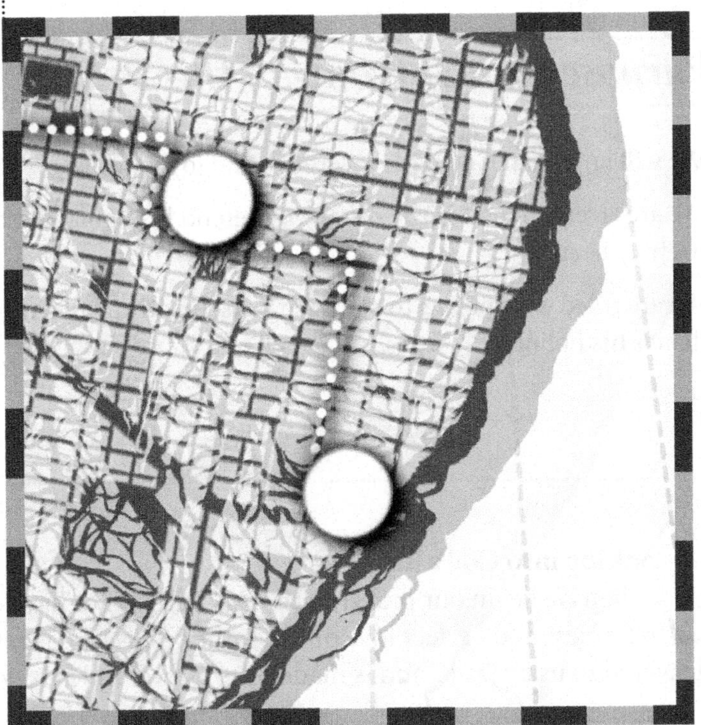

Prayer will make a man cease from sin, or sin will entice a man to cease from prayer.
John Bunyan

When we become too glib in prayer we are surely talking to ourselves.

A.W. Tozer

DAY **2**

Holy Is Your Name

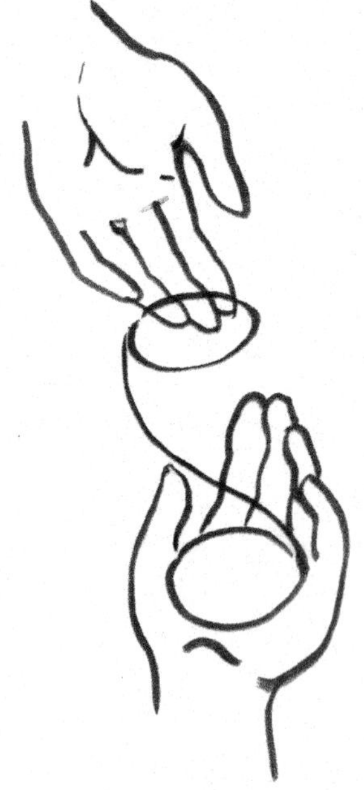

Today's Priority

* We ask to revere God's name in word, thought, and deed.
* We pray to defend and protect those who bear his image as well as those who bear his name.

Purpose and Outcome of this Prayer

* We will approach God with reverence and joy in Jesus.
* We are strengthened with courage to defend his name and to announce his holy beauty.
* We are filled with power to separate ourselves from all that opposes or denies his holiness.

Looking into God's holiness

When we begin our prayer with "Our Father" we have communion with the relentless and perfect love of the Father. This love is revealed to us in Jesus, is delivered to us by Jesus, and is made ours forever in Jesus. We now call God "Daddy"!

In this request, Jesus points us to a preeminent attribute of God – his holiness. When we pray, "Hallowed be your name," we are asking that his name would be held in honor and reverence. We pray to partake in his holiness. We pray to practice his holiness in word, thought, and deed.

We seldom pay as much attention to God's holiness as we do to his love. This is understandable. The message of Jesus and the entire New Testament is distilled into these words: "God is love."

In the Old Testament the holiness of God is highlighted. The prophet Isaiah calls God the "Holy One of Israel" twenty-seven times! In a "melt-down" vision of God, Isaiah sees and hears heaven's greatest beings, the cherubim, continually crying out:

Isaiah 6:3

> *And they were calling to one another:*
> *"Holy, holy, holy is the LORD Almighty;*
> *the whole earth is full of his glory."*

In Hebrew thought this threefold repetition is significant. God is not holy in a comparative sense, or in a superlative sense. God is holy in a super-superlative sense.

While angels and men can participate in God's holiness, he is separate from all creatures in his God-holiness.

Who is like unto you, O Lord among gods? Who is like you, majestic in holiness, awesome in glory, working wonders. *Exodus 15:11*

The holiness of God is revealed in different ways

God's holiness is rich and complex – as rich and complex as his infinite, eternal, and unchangeable being. He is holy in all that he is and does. God's holiness is revealed throughout the Bible. In this chapter, we will consider first, symbols of his holiness, second, his holy commandments, and third, the holy person of Jesus Christ. We will end by dwelling on the Holy Spirit, who is the one who makes holiness a practical reality in our lives.

1. Symbols of God's holiness

In the Old Testament there are three prominent symbols for God's holiness. These are precious jewels, blinding light, and intense fire. In one place, the prophet Ezekiel includes all three:

Above the expanse over their heads was what looked like ***a throne of sapphire****, and high above on the throne was a figure like that of a man. I saw that from what appeared to be his waist up he looked like glowing metal, as* ***if full of fire****, and that from there down he looked like fire, and* ***brilliant light surrounded him****. Like the appearance of a rainbow in the clouds on a rainy day, so was the radiance around him. This was the appearance of the likeness of the glory of the LORD. When I saw it, I fell facedown...* *Ezekiel 1:26-28*

First, precious jewels, perfect in color and clarity, indicate the purity of God. Through and through, God is pure. This purity is entrancing and beautiful. The Bible says that heaven's streets are paved with pure gold "like clear glass," its gates made of pure pearl, and its massive walls built of diamonds and jasper. This is how God describes the purity and the holiness of his kingdom. *Revelation 21:9-21*

Second, the holy presence of God radiates a brilliant light. This light is so blinding that any beholder falls down, clipped at the knees, in the presence of this glory. Mountain climbers have to wear protective lenses because of the sun's brilliance. Inuit hunters have worn dark glasses made of bone and translucent shells for centuries, in order not to go "snow blind." Anyone who sees the radiance of God's glory gropes in "light blindness." Human retinas are not made for this vision.

God is the source of all created light – spiritual and physical. Scientists now tell us that the visible universe contains some 100 billion stars in 100 billion galaxies. As we look to the heavens on a clear night, we realize that our Holy Creator God is the source of all this glorious light.

The third symbol for God's holiness is fire – a fierce, unquenchable, consuming fire. This fire warns away and draws near at the same time.

Recall how Moses is frightened by the burning bush. Yet intensely curious, he wants to get closer. In the New Testament, we are encouraged to draw near to God, but to do it "with reverence and awe, because our God is a consuming fire." *Hebrews 12:28-29* *Exodus 3:1-5*

Hebrews 12:29

In a positive sense, God's holiness is a burning passion for love, justice, righteousness, and truth. We are irresistibly drawn to this. Yet we are warned that the fire of God's holiness is destructive towards anything unholy. God's very nature is set against everything unloving, unjust, and oppressive. Anyone who ignores or despises God's name is undone when they encounter his holiness. Anyone who sets out to destroy his likeness in people he has created will encounter his perfect justice. Like a blazing fire, his being consumes any form of oppression, hatred, malice, envy, and greed.

When we put these three symbols together – precious jewels, brilliant light, and consuming fire – we are overcome by the beauty and power of God's holiness. To see God is "extreme" religion. To behold his holiness is to fall down in awe and reverence. At the same time to even get a glimpse of God's holiness is to yearn for more.

Longing for holiness

On the one hand God is separate from us in his holiness. In an absolute and qualitative sense God alone is holy. We are not holy in this sense – and never can be. On the other hand God calls us to participate in and reflect his holiness.

1 Peter 1:16 *Be holy as I am holy.*

Hebrews 12:14 *Pursue holiness, without which no one shall see the Lord.*

Our first parents, Adam and Eve, were created in innocence and holiness. When they disobeyed God they fell from this perfect state. A world fell with them:

She took. She ate. Earth felt the wound. ~Paradise Lost

Imagine all humankind hurtling along a mountain road in a bus. The bus is piloted by Adam and Eve. We begin to speed up. The brakes fail. Lurching back and forth we come to a sharp turn. We can't make it. We break the concrete barrier and plunge down the cliff. With a terrible crash we slam to a halt. Inside is a mangled mess of broken bones, bleeding, and scarred bodies. Everyone is crippled, torn, and scarred by this fall – some worse than others.

This is analogous to our spiritual nature. We are broken in the original fall of mankind. As Flannery O'Conner put it, in each of us there is "an interior dislocation of the soul." We no longer have our original holiness. Nor are we able to become holy in our own efforts. God's holy nature is now unapproachable.

However, no matter how broken and bruised, we are still irresistibly attracted to the glory and beauty of his holiness. We yearn for holiness to complete our own being. We hunger for our original fellowship with God.

This is a dilemma great enough to fill a world of tragedies. We are like moths drawn to a flame. We dare not approach the fire because we are flammable. At the same time, we cannot survive or be happy without its light and heat:

And now he began to feel a strange mixture of sensations – a sense of perfect duty to enter that secret place which the peaks were guarding combined with an equal sense of trespass. He dared not go up that pass: he dared not to do otherwise.

~*C.S. Lewis,* Perelandra

On one hand, we want to ascend to heaven and become one with God in his holiness. We are drawn in. At the same time we are not made for the journey. We are earthbound. We cannot withstand the supernova brightness or heat of his presence. We are not made of the right stuff.

We are like Icarus of the Greek myth. With his father Daedelus, Icarus was imprisoned by king Minos. They were forced to design and build the maze for the Minotar – the half man half bull who gored and devoured his prey. In order to escape, Daedelus collected feathers one at a time and made wings for himself and Icarus. He fastened them with candle wax – and warned Icarus not to fly too close to the sun, or the wings would melt. Icarus lept and flew away from the prison. He started well. However, he soon grew careless and flew too close to the sun. The wings melted and he plummeted to his death on the rocks below.

Like Icarus, we have "wings of wax." No matter how much we long to be one with God, we are not built of the stuff that permits us to fly near the brilliant burning fires of God's holiness. We are made of very flammable material.

We pray to partake in God's holiness

If God is holy through and through, and we are sinners without holiness through and through, the question is obvious. How do we reconcile these opposites? How can we fulfill our longing to draw near to God's holiness without being consumed? Isaiah asks the same question:

Who can dwell among the everlasting burnings?

Isaiah 33:14-16

Isaiah provides the answer to his own question:

He who has clean hands and a pure heart.

The solution to our need for holiness is Jesus. He is the only person since Adam and Eve born perfect in holiness. He lived a life of perfect obedience. He alone has clean hands and a pure heart. He suffered an innocent death. He is our second Adam and our second chance for a life of holiness:

For just as through the disobedience of the one man the many were made sinners, so also through the obedience of the one man the many will be made righteous.

Romans 5:19

On the cross Jesus reconciles the opposing forces of our sin and God's holiness. In him justice and mercy meet. He died to remove our sin. His death is vicarious. He is a substitute for any who will trust in him. At the moment of true belief, a believer's sin is transferred to his account. Jesus pays the debt and the one who believes is perfectly forgiven.

Not only is Jesus' death for our benefit, his life is also. He lived for us and also died for us. He died the death we could not die; he lived the life we could not live. The instant we believe, he takes our sin away. He also transfers to us the innocence and holiness of his perfect life. By faith in him we are accepted as holy before God. As if viewing his own Son, God views each pardoned child as holy:

He made him to be sin, who knew no sin, that in him we might become the righteousness of God.

2 Corinthians 5:21

Ephesians 2:6 Hebrews 4:14-16

Now we dare to approach God's holy presence – with boldness!

> *Therefore since we have a great high priest, who has passed through the heavens, Jesus, the son of God...Let us then with confidence draw near to the throne of grace, that we may receive mercy and find grace to help in our time of need.*

Forgiven of sin, covered with Jesus' innocence, now our wings are made of the right stuff! We not only ascend to God's holy presence. We live there continually: "We are now seated with Christ in the heavenly realms."

2. God's holy character is displayed in his commandments

God's holiness is revealed in the Ten Commandments. In this law we see what our holy Father requires of us and what he forbids. We see what holiness looks like when lived out in the lives of his children – in words, thoughts, and deeds.

Commands one to four are about keeping God's name holy. This is the vertical dimension of holiness. First, we are to worship God alone. Second, we are not to identify him with nature or anything man-made. Third, we are not to represent or misuse his name in any way. Fourth, we are to set aside one day in seven for worship, rest, and good works.

Commands five to ten are about honoring God's image in the people he has made. This is the horizontal dimension. Fifth, we are to honor our parents. Sixth to tenth, we are forbidden to kill, commit adultery, steal, falsely accuse, or envy our neighbour. In a positive way we are actively to preserve and protect our neighbor's life, spouse, property, and reputation.

A genuine concern and love for God's name always leads us to pray for and serve all those who bear his image and carry his name. Praise of God leads to prayer for people.

Because each of us is made in God's image, God's holy likeness is in every human being. In this sense, everyone represents him and bears his name. Every man, woman, and child, no matter how broken and bruised by the fall, still bears the mark of his image and must be loved and honored for God's sake. Our concern for the name of God results in love and concern for our fellow man.

Our concern for others is intensified in the case of those who are called by God's name. Christians are simply those who love Jesus and wear his name – the name "Christian." Our zeal for God's name is multiplied in holy concern and prayer for everyone who bears Jesus' name in the world.

3. Supremely, the holiness of God is revealed in Jesus Christ

Jesus is holy. He lived a perfect life and died a perfect death. Jesus kept all the commandments – the prohibitions and requirements, the commandments towards God and towards man, and the commandments of inner intent and of just action.

Jesus reveals the full glory and holiness of God, in person, and in his very nature. Notice how John the apostle describes Jesus' holy life in the same symbols and language used of God:

John 1:4,5,14,17

> *In him was life, and that life was **the light of men**. The light shines in the darkness, but the darkness has not understood it...The Word became flesh and made his*

dwelling among us. We have seen his glory, ***the glory of the One and Only,*** *who came from the Father,* ***full of grace and truth****...For the law was given through Moses; grace and truth came through Jesus Christ. No one has ever seen God, but God the One and Only, who is at the Father's side, has made him known.*

Just as the sun is inseparable from its effulgence of light and heat, Jesus is the pure and blinding radiance of God. Jesus said, "I am the light of the world." The apostle Paul went blind for three days when he saw Jesus in his ascended glory. In Revelation we read about the ascended Jesus, that his face is like "the sun shining in full strength."

John 8:12
Acts 9:9
Revelation 1:16

Therefore, it is Jesus who supremely reveals and defines holiness for the believer. Holiness is not just a matter of keeping commandments. Holiness involves following Jesus and becoming like Jesus. For a believer, holiness is not legislative – it is personal and relational. In Biblical thought, our renewal in God's holiness always involves becoming like Jesus:

Do not lie to each other, since you have taken off your old self with its practices and have put on the new self, which ***is being renewed in knowledge in the image of its Creator****. Here there is no Greek or Jew, circumcised or uncircumcised, barbarian, Scythian, slave or free, but* ***Christ is all, and is in all.***

Colossians 3:9-11

When we pray for God's help to live holy lives he will give us power to do so

Now that we live in the presence and power of Jesus, who loved us and died for us, we are able to participate in the holiness of God. The apostle Peter writes, "We have become partakers in the divine nature." We are covered in Christ's innocence and righteousness and can enjoy the holiness of God.

2 Peter 1:4

Through prayer and the Holy Spirit, we are being restored to a holy life – like the holy life Jesus lived among us. This is a life-long process called sanctification. "Sanctification" is Latin for "becoming holy."

The gift of Christ's holiness is like a seed sown into the human heart. In time the seed sprouts, grows, and bears leaves and fruit. As each believer receives the grace of Christ's righteousness, they are gradually transformed into the likeness of Christ himself.

We cannot impart holiness to ourselves. We cannot keep God's commandments or be like Jesus on our own. The good news is not only that Jesus lived and died as our substitute – he now gives the Holy Spirit to live within the very heart of every believer:

Those who are led by the Spirit of God are sons of God. For you did not receive a spirit that makes you a slave again to fear, but you received the Spirit of sonship. And by him we cry, "Abba, Father." The Spirit himself testifies with our spirit that we are God's children.

Romans 8:14-16

The Christian life is impossible apart from the Holy Spirit. We are no more able to be holy in our own strength than we are able to leap through the stratosphere and escape the earth's gravity. In our fallen nature we are too weak. The gravity of this world's sin is too great.

Ephesians 5:18

In order to break through the force of gravity a rocket requires an upward thrust of seventeen thousand miles per hour. This requires rocket fuel. To overcome the immense gravity of our weakness and sin we need more than natural power. We need supernatural power. This is why Jesus promises to give us his Holy Spirit. This is why we ask continually to "be filled with the Holy Spirit."

It is because of the power and presence of the Holy Spirit that we are able to say "No!" to the temptations of the world and the corruptions of our own nature.

Romans 8:13

> *For if you live according to the sinful nature, you will die; but if by the Spirit you put to death the misdeeds of the body, you will live.*

It is because of the gift of the Holy Spirit that we are able to step out of our selfishness and devote ourselves to serving others.

When we pray, "Hallowed be your name," we ask for power. When we do, we will be filled with the courage and strength needed for a life of holiness. This is what happened to the early church, and it will happen again today. Consider this remarkable example from the book of Acts:

Acts 4:24,31-35

> *When they heard this, they raised their voices together in prayer to God... After they prayed, the place where they were meeting was shaken. And they were all filled with the Holy Spirit and spoke the word of God boldly.*
>
> *All the believers were one in heart and mind. No one claimed that any of his possessions was his own, but they shared everything they had. With great power the apostles continued to testify to the resurrection of the Lord Jesus, and much grace was upon them all. There were no needy persons among them. For from time to time those who owned lands or houses sold them, brought the money from the sales and put it at the apostles' feet, and it was distributed to anyone as he had need.*

What a wonderful change from the selfishness and pride characterizing the disciples before receiving the Holy Spirit. A radical and generous sharing of possessions; boldly speaking out about Jesus' resurrection; a deep sense of restored and empowered relationship with God – they were filled with the Holy Spirit. This is what it means to follow Jesus. This is what holiness is all about.

Supremely, "hallowed be your name" is a call to worship God as we pray

When we think of worship we might think only about Sunday morning. However, there are two kinds of worship in the Bible. The first denotes a life of worship. In this sense we are to offer our words, thoughts, and deeds in a daily way to God:

Romans 12:1,2

> *Therefore, I urge you, brothers, in view of God's mercy, to offer your bodies as living sacrifices, holy and pleasing to God – **this is your spiritual act of worship**. Do not conform any longer to the pattern of this world, but be transformed by the renewing of your mind.*

It is only when we carry out this general and daily worship that Sunday morning worship has any meaning or authenticity.

The second kind of worship is praising, proclaiming, and singing the wonders of God's person and his actions. Like the angels, we are to sing:

Holy, Holy, Holy, is the Lord God Almighty.

Isaiah 6:3

Joining heaven's choirs we sing,

Who is like unto you, O lord among gods?
Who is like unto you, glorious in holiness, awesome in praises, doing wonders?

Exodus 15:7

This is where our prayer ultimately leads and finds its fulfillment – to joyous praise of God.

DAY 

Prayerful Pondering

Questions for Reflection

* What is your attitude in coming to God in prayer? How much are your prayers characterized by a sense of worship?

* Where in the world around you do you wish for God's holiness and justice to break through? Where do you need courage to stand for righteousness and justice?

Summary of Key Idea(s) *What key thought(s) do you want to remember or revisit?*

Prayer Prompts: *Use these points to guide your prayers. Try writing out your prayers.*

When we pray "holy is your name":

* With reverence, we worship and honour God for his beauty and purity.
* We tremble with thanksgiving for the great price Jesus paid for our unrighteousness, so that we can be in relationship with our holy God.
* We ask for power, courage, and strength needed for a life of holiness personally and in the world around us.

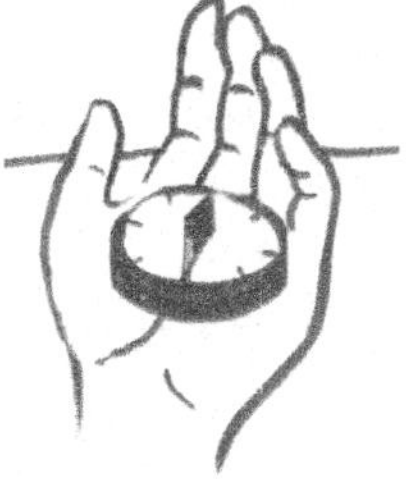

Prayer Practice

Try practicing worshiping God in prayer – before you ask for anything.

DAY **2**

Prayer Practice:
Preparing for a Daily Pattern for Prayer

Overview

Throughout this book, we will lead you through a pattern and sequence for prayer that focuses on one priority from Jesus' prayer each day. Today you will apply the pattern to "Holy is your name."

Pattern for Prayer ► *Applied to "Holy is your name"*

1 **Priority & Promise**

Praise God for his promises & priorities

Start by focusing on the priority **UPWARD to God.** Allow the Holy Spirit to guide you through the priority for the day.

Praise Jesus for the priority. Meditate on **what it means,** what it reveals about God, about Jesus' passion and purpose.

* *Spend some time worshiping God. Don't ask for anything. Simply ponder who he is. Contemplate his holiness. Take joy in Jesus.*

2 **Passions**

Pray God's promises & priorities into **your own heart**

Next pray the priority **INWARD into your heart.** Talk with God about your present heart state, allowing him to thoroughly examine and encourage you.

Ask Jesus to **transform your heart** and life to be more like his.

* *Ask God to examine your heart regarding his holiness. Thank God for growth in worship and reverence of him in your life. Confess sinful attitudes, thoughts, or habits that dishonour God.*

3 **People**

Pray God's promises as a **blessing to others**

Now pray **OUTWARD for others to experience more of God**'s promises.

Pray for **people,** your loved ones, other individuals, ministries, your church, city, and the world.

* *Pray for God's people to have an authentic life of worship that honours God. Pray for God's holy name to be defended.*

* *Pray for God's holiness and justice to break through in your city and world around you.*

4 **Praise**

Praise God for all his blessings

End by **praising God** for his blessings and answers to prayer.

Recall how God has been present. Remember to **thank** him.

* *Praise God for his holiness. Thank him for answers, blessings, or insights he reveals to you in your prayers.*

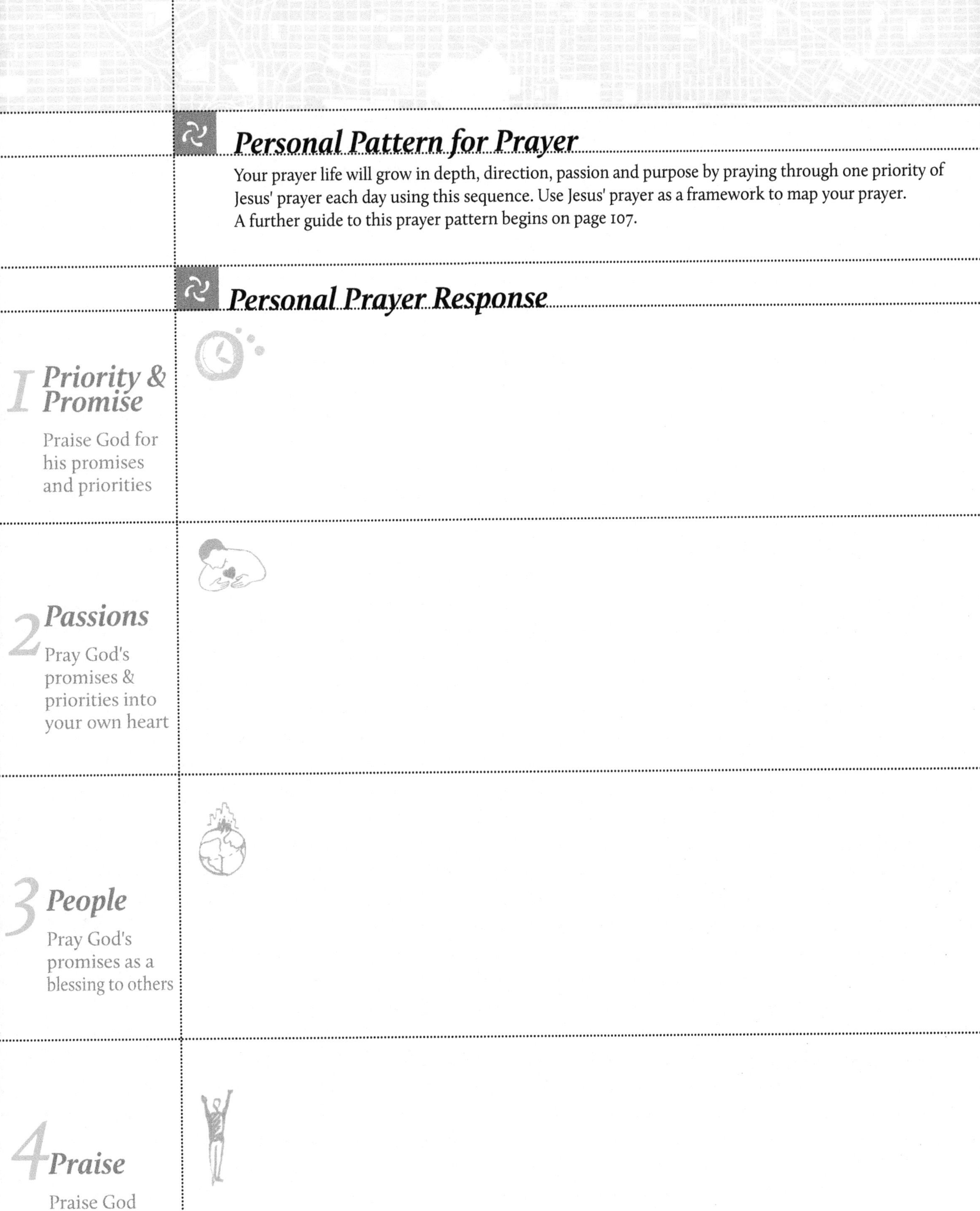

Personal Pattern for Prayer

Your prayer life will grow in depth, direction, passion and purpose by praying through one priority of Jesus' prayer each day using this sequence. Use Jesus' prayer as a framework to map your prayer. A further guide to this prayer pattern begins on page 107.

Personal Prayer Response

1 *Priority & Promise*

Praise God for his promises and priorities

2 *Passions*

Pray God's promises & priorities into your own heart

3 *People*

Pray God's promises as a blessing to others

4 *Praise*

Praise God for all his blessings

Your Kingdom Come

DAY 1 2 **3** 4 5 6 7

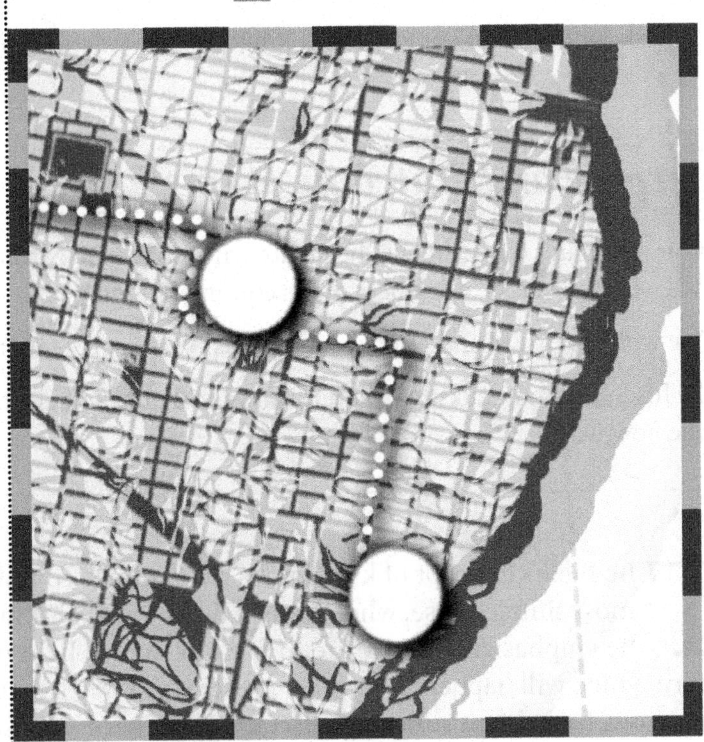

To clasp the hands in prayer is the beginning of an uprising against the disorder of the world.
Karl Barth

So that your prayer may have its full weight with God, see that you be in charity with all men... Nor can you expect to receive any blessing from God while you have not charity towards your neighbor.
Richard Sibbes

DAY 3

Your Kingdom Come

Today's Priority

* In this petition we give our allegiance to Jesus as our present and coming king.
* We pray for Jesus to rule and reign in our hearts by his Spirit.
* We eagerly await and prepare for his second coming and the renewal of all things.
* We ask for others to come into his kingdom by faith in Jesus.

Purpose and Outcome of this Prayer

* Our inner and outer life will be created and shaped according to his coming kingdom. We will walk to the drumbeat of his coming kingdom.
* We will be faithful and effective in witness to our present and coming king.
* By his Spirit and grace, here and now, we live out the cultural mandate of the new world.

The Bible's concept of kingdom is rich but not complicated. In its most simple sense, when Jesus tells us to pray "Your kingdom come," he emphasizes that we are to live our lives in light of his triumphant return which will happen at the end of the world. We live today in light of tomorrow. No present suffering, discouragement, or opposition can overcome our confident hope that Jesus will soon restore all things.

According to the New Testament, Jesus is the king of his people and of the entire world. Yet Jesus' kingdom does not come all at once. His kingdom comes in stages.

To begin with, Jesus is our "Forever King." As the second person of the Trinity, Jesus has always ruled and reigned with the Father and Holy Spirit. The apostle John writes:

John 1: 1-3

In the beginning was the word.
The word was with God and the word was God.
He was in the beginning with God.
Through him all things were made that have been made.
In him was life, and that life was the light of men.

Second, when Jesus lived and died for us, he became our "Redeemer King." His death is an inauguration and his resurrection is a coronation. In Paul's letter to the Philippian Christians, Paul writes:

Being found in appearance as a man, he humbled himself and became obedient to death – even death on a cross! Therefore God exalted him to the highest place and has given him the name that is above every name, that at the name of Jesus every knee should bow, in heaven and on earth and under the earth, and every tongue confess that Jesus Christ is Lord.

Philippians 2:8-11

Third, Jesus is our "Coming King," as the one who will judge and recreate all things at the end of the world. Jesus promises that he will return and he will vindicate his faithful followers and reveal the injustice of those who reject him:

At that time the sign of the Son of Man will appear in the sky, and all the nations of the earth will mourn. They will see the Son of Man coming on the clouds of the sky, with power and great glory. And he will send his angels with a loud trumpet call, and they will gather his elect from the four winds, from one end of the heavens to the other.

Matthew 24:30,31

Jesus' kingdom is coming in a final sense because he is coming again to renew the entire creation and to bring in the new age.

We put these three aspects of Jesus' kingship together when we pray "Your kingdom come." We pray as loyal subjects who acknowledge his eternal creator-lordship. We pray as those who accept his saving work in his incarnation. We cry out in eager expectation of his coming again to renew all things.

A modern day metaphor

In our democratic and egalitarian culture we may find it difficult to relate to the hierarchy and majesty involved in the concept of kingdom. An illustration can help. We can use a contemporary business metaphor to make these concepts relevant.

Imagine a Fortune 500 company buying out and taking over a smaller company which has fallen on hard times. It happens all the time.

The takeover company is Dominion Realty. It is a massive company with offices and operations all over the country. Dominion buys out Independent Realty – a smaller company.

The day after takeover, the Dominion boss forms a transition team of managers. Their task is simple. He gives these instructions, "I give you three years to make Independent into a Dominion company. I do not want to chop this company up. I want to renew and rebuild it. Keep as many employees and managers as possible. Win them over if you can. At the end of three years I am coming to see what you have done."

He ends his instructions with finality and clarity: "You know my expectations. You know my values. Anytime you need my help just call. I will give anything you need. Now go to work!"

While both Dominion and Independent are in the real estate business, they have different ways of doing things. They are different cultures. Dominion is about team work. Independent values individual accomplishments above everything. Dominion is about profit sharing. Independent rewards entrepreneurs and pressure sales. At Dominion they look after the little guy. There is employee training and support. They are reluctant to let someone go once they hire them. At Independent, the philosophy is, "pull your weight or you're dead weight." Dominion is concerned about company culture. Independent is concerned about the bottom line.

The transition team arrives on site and gets to know Independent. After a month of careful listening, they gather everyone together to make an announcement. Corinne is the spokesperson.

She starts by stating the situation in simple terms, "You are already a Dominion company. You have been bought lock, stock, and barrel by our boss. At the end of three years the boss is coming and this company has to be a Dominion company."

Corrine adds some good news, "We are going to have a Dominion company. Nothing can stop that. But don't think for a minute we want to get rid of you! This is not a hostile takeover. We want to win you over. Dominion is a great company with a great boss. If you are willing to get on board you can be part of a fantastic future for you and your family. If not, you will probably quit before we have to let you go."

She finishes, "Bottom line, the boss is coming soon. He knows what he wants. Whatever remains to be done, he will quickly finish when he gets here. Our only job is to get ready for his coming."

Getting ready for the return of the King

How does this illustration relate to the coming kingdom of God?

Jesus is the Dominion boss. This world, insofar as it does not acknowledge his present lordship, is "Independent." The time between his first and second coming is the three year transition.

As Christians we are the transition management team. We have a job to do. We announce the reality of the situation. The king has come. His imperial takeover is finished. It was completed at the cross. It was ratified by his resurrection. In military terms – the war is over. Every enemy has been defeated. Any remaining skirmishes indicate ignorance or a stubborn reluctance to accept this. Surrender is an accomplished fact. All that remains is a formal session to ratify the terms.

We announce that our king is coming again. This second coming is unstoppable. It is certain. It is final. It will be total. It is our job as Christians and the job of any who join us, to arrange everything to prepare for that coming.

As his servant-messengers we realize this world is going to be remade. Jesus has the blueprint and agenda. From the day of his resurrection "takeover" things are changing. Over his entire realm he is winning converts and allies. Our chief business, and most enjoyable task, is to win people over for our coming king.

During this interim period, we not only announce that Jesus is coming, we teach and carry out the plans and priorities of our coming king. We have his word. We have his example. We have his clear commands and promises. We know how things are going to be.

We live out the priorities of the future kingdom today. We make plans and take decisive steps to transform our present society into tomorrow's likeness. Someone said, "Christians are building show homes. Their job is to show what the new neighborhood will look like."

Returning to our illustration, let's see what happens after Corrine's announcement.

To begin with, there are some who want nothing to do with the Dominion takeover. The Independent boss does not take long to make his views known. "With all these changing rules and values how can anyone get work done around here? Everything we have worked so hard for is being ruined!"

Everyone loyal to the old boss, and those who most profited in the pre-Dominion order, get his drift. They begin to grumble too.

Before long the old boss quits. He moves to the other side of town and sets up a competitive company. He drops hints and leaves the door open for others to join him. The new Independent team has a new mission. It is not only to restart Independent. The new goal is to overthrow Dominion – alleging a "hostile-takeover" as the pretext. With renewed passion, Independent engines are stoked to high intensity.

However, other Independent employees are willing to take a look at the new company. Most are tired of the overtime. Only a few reaped any significant rewards from the old ways. Most of them lived on low wages and were in constant concern about job security. Due to firings and exhaustion, there is a high turnover in staff.

The Dominion team wants to reverse this trend. Peter, who is on the transition team comes up to Jim, an account manager for Independent. The conversation goes like this:

"Jim, I notice you let Frank go last week. What was the problem? He seemed to be working hard. He was pleasant enough."

Jim answers, "Yeah he tried. But he couldn't cut it. He made a lot of mistakes. He took too many hours to do his work."

Peter paused – reflecting for a minute, "Jim, I want you to give Frank another chance. Let's tell him the situation. Let's get him some training if he needs it. He seems to have a good attitude. I think we can make progress."

"Okay. You're the boss."

"Actually I'm not. I just work for him – like you!

"By the way Jim, I notice you let six or seven others go in the past six months. I wonder if we shouldn't call them up too."

Eyebrows raised, Jim stares at Peter.

"I'll tell you what. Call them and offer them their old job back. Offer them a chance to become a part of Dominion. Tell them, if they are willing so are we."

Jim asks, "What gives here? What kind of company is this? Who wants to keep everyone on payroll and even hire people back? I don't get it."

Peter just smiled. He could see things from Jim's perspective.

"I can understand your confusion Jim. I didn't understand at first either. You see, it's our boss. He likes to rebuild things. He likes to make winners out of losers."

He continued, "You see, when our boss was younger, he went through hell. He suffered a personal catastrophe. Everyone thought he was finished. No one gave him a chance."

"Anyway, somehow, he came back. It happened suddenly – you might say miraculously. One day he's down, the next he's on top of the world. That very day he starts to change everything – and I mean everything! That's why he loves the little guy. That's why he always gives a second chance. He is all about a fresh start."

Jim listens. "Interesting. But what about you? What gives with you?"

"I'm glad you asked. Well, I was a workaholic. I put work first. I said it was for the family, but in my heart I knew it was about me. It was about my need to succeed. Anyway, it cost me everything. I lost my wife. She gave up on me. My kids too. Even my business went under."

"I was a useless wreck when the boss found me. One day he called me out of nowhere. He asked if I wanted to do some transition work. He thought I might be good at it. He gave me another chance. Now I get to help other shipwrecks like myself. I get to offer them a new start. I have a new purpose – and it feels good, really worthwhile. "

"Okay, that makes some sense. But what about the others on your team. What's their story?"

"Pretty much similar to mine."

"What about Corrine? How did she get to be the spokesperson?"

Peter thought about it for a minute, "She was doing well until she got married. She thought she married for love. Unfortunately, her husband loved to abuse her. When she finally left him, she was down for the count. She quit her high paying job and was looking at fast food joints for work. The boss found her and gave her a job. She quickly became the team leader."

Jim asked, "What about Phil? He seems nice enough – but why is he always grimacing?"

"Ah, Phil. Another great story. I know he tends to grimace. About nine months ago, he was diagnosed with cancer. He's dying. It's already shot through every part of his lymph system. There's no cure. His number is up. Two months ago his company let him go. They didn't have money to keep him. He left with a small severance and no insurance. Doom was written all over him."

"The boss calls him up. He says, 'Phil, I know you don't want to rust out. How would you like to go out in a blaze? I have one last job for you if you want it.' Well here he is. Going out in a blaze!" Jim thought he saw tears welling up in Peter's eyes. Yes, definitely. He was crying.

Before leaving Peter says, "You see, Jim, this is not just a job. It's more of a mission. It's about appreciation. It's about loyalty. Frankly, I love the boss. He could ask me to shovel manure and I would – in a minute!"

A little miffed by all this intensity and passion, Jim didn't say anything. He didn't know what to say.

Sharing our story

Taking our cue from Peter, we can understand some dynamics of Jesus' coming kingdom. Sharing what Jesus has done for us is not just a job. It's about loyalty to our coming king. It's about looking forward to seeing him again.

Each child of God gets to live a second life. Our old life dies the day Jesus takes over. While we wait for his return we share our story. We explain to others how Jesus has established the kingdom of God once and for all.

We explain that God owns every last atom, proton, and electron in the universe. He rules every star, galaxy, quasar, and black hole. He is the creator-king and every man, woman, and child owes him worship and thanks. He is king of all kings. Every politician, educator, parent, and employer gets their authority from him and will give him an account of their work:

> *He is the head over every power and authority. Having disarmed the powers and authorities, he made a public spectacle over them, triumphing over them by the cross...He is the beginning and first born from the dead, so that in everything he might have supremacy.*

Colossians 2:10,15

> *Then I heard every creature in heaven and on earth and under the earth and on the sea, and all that is in them, singing: "To him who sits on the throne, and to the Lamb be praise and honor and glory and power, for ever and ever!"*

Revelations 5:13

Some Christians are embarrassed by this apocalyptic message. Talking about the end of the world seems foreboding - even frightening. However, we need to remember, this "ending" is a great beginning. Jesus' coming is not about the end of all things. It is about a beginning. All the history of this world is only a brief introduction, merely the cover of a book, introducing a far greater story. We haven't even gotten to the good stuff yet. In the rest of the book, sorrow, sickness, tears, and death will be left behind. Hatred, violence, and oppression will burn up in the nova heat of his coming. Everything that is good remains. What is weak becomes strong. Small fragments of precious faith are refined and perfected. Best of all, anyone who wants to start fresh and to live forever in unimaginable bliss is welcome to become a part of his new world. We get to pass out the invitations!

We learn to share our story with humility. His bright and strong grace is written on the dark background of our lives. We are redeemed - but we are redeemed sinners. As one poet writes, we were found among "scattered shards of broken lives."

Living out the values of the kingdom

There is more to the kingdom than telling others about Jesus' first and second coming. We also ask for his grace and Spirit to live out the values and character of his coming kingdom today. We look for our present world to change, in our communities and cities, as a result of his kingdom coming into our lives.

Remember what the boss said to his transition team. He tells them he wants to change the values and way of doing things in this company, "I want a Dominion company when I come back."

While the Dominion transition team is winning over Independent employees, they are still in business! With Independent employees they share a common workplace, a common market, and a common task. They do not come in to end the doing of business. They come to end the way business is done.

This is true of Jesus' transition team too. With neighbors, friends, and family we share a common environment, a common political system, the same economy. Though we have a new king, we live in the same communities, go to the same schools, and work in the same marketplace. We share the same social needs.

We live in cities and communities with the poor, elderly, shut-in, infirm, abandoned, new immigrants, addicts, and victims of abuse and exploitation. We know "down and outers." We know "up and outers." We know "way-outers" too. When we pray "Your kingdom come," we daily apply our prayers to the deep needs of our cities.

An example in Vancouver

In our city of Vancouver, Lorne Epp directs *More Than a Roof* Housing Society. This Christian ministry works with local and civic leaders to build and maintain quality single resident accommodations. The goal is to help the impoverished and mentally ill by giving them the dignity of their own place to live.

Through prayer we share the almightiness of God... Christians who pray are helpers and saviors, yea, masters and gods of the world. They are the legs which bear the world.
Martin Luther

Lorne came into this line of ministry after his family had to commit a great deal of time, resource, and love to helping one of their own family members who struggled with mental illness. It took everything this family had to keep this loved one off of the streets. Jesus used this time to prepare Lorne for helping others in similar circumstances. *More Than a Roof* now serves hundreds of needy people in Vancouver. They may be on hard times, they may struggle with mental illness, they may be recovering from addictions – all are welcome. All are given the dignity of a home to live in.

Lorne puts it this way, "Christians need to remember the great commandment as well as the great commission. Jesus taught us to love our neighbor as well as to lead him to faith." The theme verse of Lorne's life highlights the implications of Jesus' first and second coming:

Is this not the kind of fast I have chosen...
Is it not to share your food with the hungry and to provide the poor wanderer with shelter – when you see the naked, to clothe him...
Your people will rebuild the ancient ruins and will raise the age old foundations; you will be called Repairer of Broken Walls, Restorer of Streets with Dwellings."

Isaiah 58:6,7,12

We are saved by faith alone, but not by a faith that is alone. The outcome of genuine faith will always be a life of kindness, justice, and good works.

This applies directly to our prayer, "Your kingdom come."

Prayer is socially revolutionary because it prepares the way for the advance of the gospel in society, and the gospel carries with it new social values that contain the seeds for a new society based on the righteousness of the kingdom.
DONALD BLOESCH

Let's return to our story.

Jim from accounting is almost ready to sign on and join Dominion for good. He has one more important question to ask. He walks up to Peter and asks, "Peter, tell me. Where do you get your energy and resolve to keep going? Frankly, I want some of that."

Peter smiled, "Jim, each of us has a direct line to the boss. If you want you can have one too. He tells each of us to call him day or night for any reason whatever. And you know what? It may seem strange, but he always answers. I never get voice-mail or call forwarding. When I do get a hold of him, he never seems in a rush. I can't remember him ever ending the conversation. It gets a little awkward sometimes, but after a while I just have to say 'goodbye.' He says 'Okay, but call back soon.'"

Like Peter, God's children have a direct line too. The direct line is prayer. We have unlimited personal and direct access to our father for his friendship, strength and wisdom. There is no obstacle that we cannot face with him at our side. There is no challenge we cannot overcome by his grace and presence through prayer.

Postscript

At the end of three years the boss comes back. It is the end of a busy week. Everyone is at the office to pick up their paycheck. Unannounced, he enters from the back. He walks towards the front office. It is pretty obvious who he is. As one employee said, "You just kind of know."

Everyone has been waiting for this day. Most stop and stare. As he goes through the offices he starts to smile. He has a feel for things, and things feel good. He comes into the front office, looks at his transition team and the other leaders. Peter, Corrine, Ted, and Phil look excited and a bit nervous at the same time. Jim feels weak at the knees.

He asks these leaders to come out so he can talk to everyone. His transition team is at the front. With a deep and genuine smile he says, "I like what I see. It feels good here. It feels like a Dominion company. I am really happy each of you is here. You are obviously doing your work. You are becoming a real team."

He turns to face Corrine and the other leaders, "Corrine, Peter, Ted, Phil – you have done it again! Good work. Tell me, was I right or what? It's been a blast hasn't it?"

He turns and looks at Jim, "Oh, and you Jim. From the day I bought Independent I knew you were going to be a part of us. What took you so long? Welcome home."

He adds, "I'll tell you guys what. First thing on Monday I want you to introduce share options for every employee. Give them a part of the organization. I want them to get a share of our success. As for you that led this transition, and Jim too, this location is yours to run for me. Enjoy it. I know you will do a great job. You have already proven it."

I hope the point is clear. Our greatest joy as believers will be to see the face of Jesus when he comes in his glory. There will be no mistaking him in that day. We will be eager and anxious for him to give his verdict on our work. When we pray "Your kingdom come", we pray to be ready for that day. We ask to hear,

Matthew 25:23

"Well done good and faithful servant. You have been faithful with a few things; I will put you in charge of many things. Come and share your master's happiness."

DAY 3

Prayerful Pondering

Questions for Reflection

* Where in your life do you experience tension between Independent and Dominion values?

* Jesus gives you unlimited personal and direct access to the Father for friendship, strength and wisdom. Where do you need his strength, and wisdom to live by Dominion values in your own life?

* How are you preparing for the boss' return?

Summary of Key Idea(s) *What key thought(s) do you want to remember or revisit?*

Prayer Prompts: *Use these points to guide your prayers. Try writing out your prayers.*

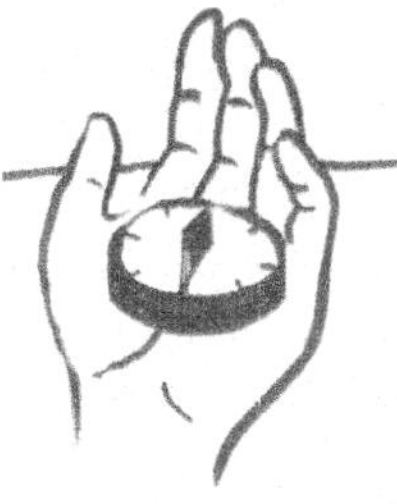

When we pray "Your kingdom come":

* We give our loyalty to Jesus and acknowledge his creator lordship and leadership in our lives. We ask to be used to lead others to know Jesus too.
* We cry out in eager expectation of his coming again to renew all things. We pray for the deep needs of our city, for his values of restoration, and rebuilding to reign.
* We ask for the Spirit, grace, courage, and wisdom to live out the values and character of Jesus' coming kingdom today.

DAY **3**

Prayer Practice:
Preparing for a Daily Pattern for Prayer

Overview

Throughout this book, we will lead you through a pattern and sequence for prayer that focuses on one priority from Jesus' prayer each day. Today you will apply the pattern to "your kingdom come."

Pattern for Prayer ►

1 **Priority & Promise**

Praise God for his promises & priorities

Start by focusing on the priority **UPWARD to God.** Allow the Holy Spirit to guide you through the priority for the day.

Praise Jesus for the priority. Meditate on **what it means,** what it reveals about God, about Jesus' passion and purpose.

2 **Passions**

Pray God's promises & priorities into **your own heart**

Next pray the priority **INWARD into your heart.** Talk with God about your present heart state, allowing him to thoroughly examine and encourage you.

Ask Jesus to **transform your heart** and life to be more like his.

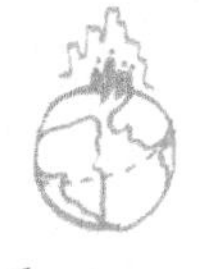

3 **People**

Pray God's promises as a **blessing to others**

Now pray **OUTWARD for others to experience more of God**'s promises.

Pray for **people,** your loved ones, other individuals, ministries, your church, city, and the world.

4 **Praise**

Praise God for all his blessings

End by **praising God** for his blessings and answers to prayer.

Recall how God has been present. Remember to **thank** him.

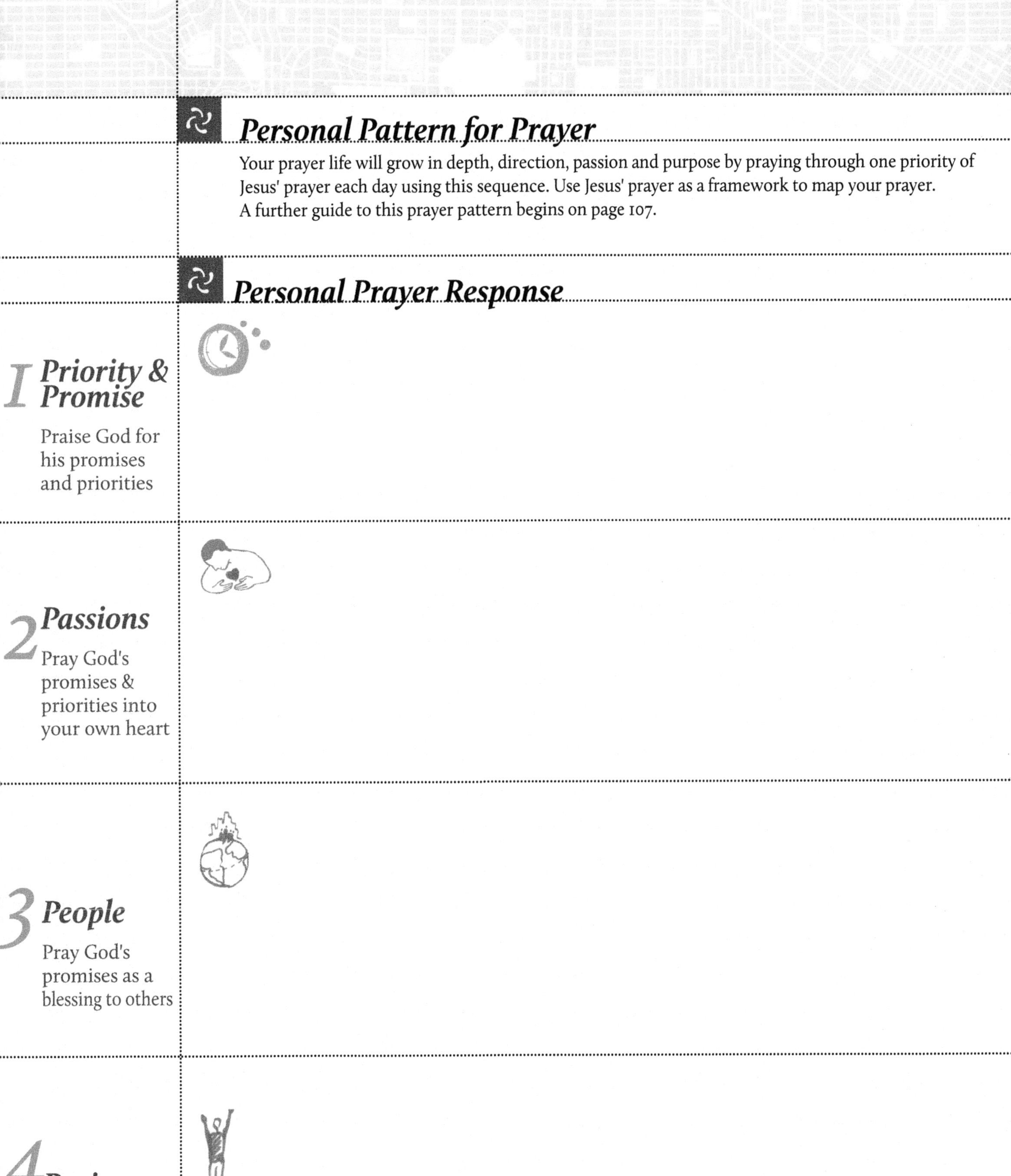

Personal Pattern for Prayer

Your prayer life will grow in depth, direction, passion and purpose by praying through one priority of Jesus' prayer each day using this sequence. Use Jesus' prayer as a framework to map your prayer. A further guide to this prayer pattern begins on page 107.

Personal Prayer Response

1 *Priority & Promise*

Praise God for his promises and priorities

2 *Passions*

Pray God's promises & priorities into your own heart

3 *People*

Pray God's promises as a blessing to others

4 *Praise*

Praise God for all his blessings

Your Will Be Done

ON EARTH AS IT IS IN HEAVEN

DAY 1 2 3 **4** 5 6 7

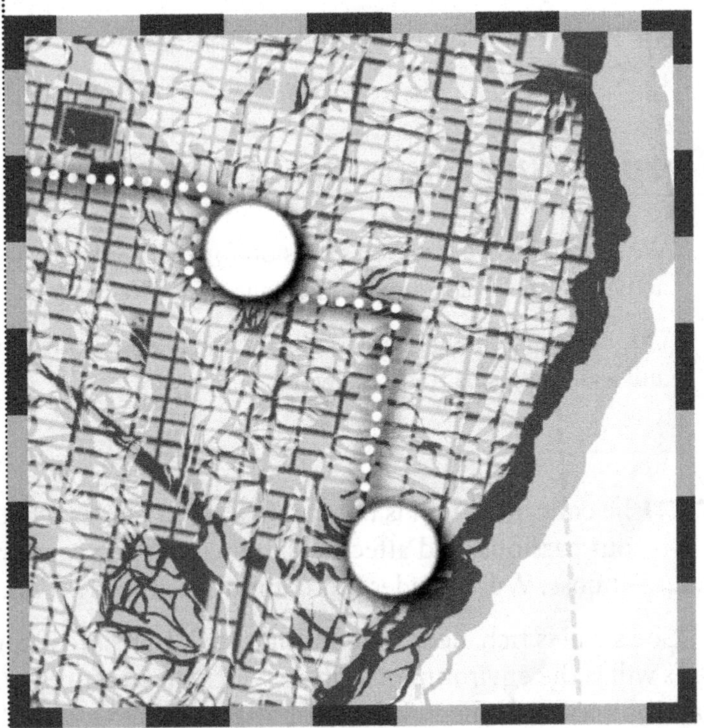

The purpose of prayer is not to get man's will done in heaven, but to get God's will done on earth.
WARREN WIERSBE

Prayer transforms our vision and makes us see it in the light of God.
THOMAS MERTON

The purpose of all prayer is to find God's will and to make that will our prayer.
CATHERINE MARSHALL

DAY 4

Your Will Be Done

ON EARTH AS IT IS IN HEAVEN

Today's Priority

* Today we seek to accept God's will, to approve God's will, and to do God's will.
* We ask to share his passion for justice and righteousness.
* We pray for compassion for the oppressed and mercy towards oppressors.
* We thank Jesus for his suffering against injustice.

Purpose and Outcome of this Prayer

* We share and live out God's passion for social justice; we become active agents of God's redeeming agenda as we pray.
* Our cities are changed as God hears and answers our prayers, and as he sends us to do his work.

The concept of will is not simple. Will includes what we desire, our passions, and affections. It includes our capacity and freedom to choose. Will includes our commitment to right and wrong.

God's will is rich, deep and multifaceted. In its most comprehensive sense, God's will is the environment within which all creatures exist. When Jesus asserts that God's will is "done in heaven," he means that God's will is the symphony to which all heaven and its myriad of angelic hosts are tuned. This music is so vast and deep and rich that all the songs of heaven are a part of it. God creates the world "while the morning stars sang together and all the angels shout for joy." Think of the world's great symphonies – *The Planets, The Pastoral Symphony, The Four Seasons.* Throw in Purcell's *Trumpet Voluntary*. Imagine all rolled into one harmonious, beautiful, and joyous song.

Job 38:7

We are to do God's will on earth "as it is in heaven" because God's angels in heaven are in perfect harmony with God's will. Thousands and thousands of angels are in "joyful assembly" because they are tuned to God's will. The cherubim – awesome angelic beings who surround God's throne – are so tuned to God's will that their very movements are in synch with God, so that "wherever the Spirit would go they would go."

Hebrews 12:22

Ezekiel 1:20

If we are to carry out God's will on earth as in heaven, it is more than a matter of simple obedience. We need to share the angels' inner harmony with the will of God. Our wills need to be tuned to God's will. This is the transformational goal of this command. The apostle Paul points us in this direction:

Do not conform any longer to the pattern of this world, but be transformed by the renewing of your mind. Then you will be able to test and approve what God's will is – his good pleasing and perfect will.

Romans 12:1-3

In contrast with heaven "on earth" his will is not done. From earliest history, there is a dissonance on earth because we have edited God from the songs of our lives. This dissonance manifests itself as exploitation, propaganda, violence, cruelty, and all other forms of injustice. It has spread through all places through all history.

Yet God does not surrender his song to this discord. He renews the concert of his will – his perfect plan and purpose – to centre stage in history. When Jesus comes to the stable in Bethlehem, on earth we hear heaven's music once again:

Suddenly a great company of the heavenly host appeared with the angel, praising God and saying, "Glory to God in the highest, and on earth peace to men on whom his favor rests."

Luke 2:13, 14

When Jesus surrenders his life on a Roman cross, we imagine a song of lament and funeral eulogy, as the earth itself groans and the skies mourn in darkness. This song is so heart-rending and sorrowful that to hear it is to remember it forever.

DAY 4

When Jesus rises from the dead, we spring from the minor key. We hear the pizzicato of the strings, the dance of the woodwinds and uproarious thunder of the percussion. Our hearts leap and creation dances to the triumphant chorus. This song spreads in overwhelming joy and healing, "as far as the curse is found."

Sing to the LORD a new song; sing to the LORD, all the earth.

Sing to the LORD, praise his name; proclaim his salvation day after day.

Let the heavens rejoice, let the earth be glad; let the sea resound, and all that is in it,

Let the fields be jubilant, and everything in them. Then all the trees of the forest will sing for joy;

They will sing before the LORD, for he comes, he comes to judge the earth. He will judge the world in righteousness and the peoples in his truth.

Psalm 96:1,2,11,13

When we pray, "your will be done on earth as it is in heaven," we are asking to once again hear the symphony of God's will. We want to tune our lives to this music and to become a joyous part of its song. We want to obey God, but we want to do it with a song of joy and thanks in our heart.

The scope of this prayer

When we ask that "your will be done on earth as it is in heaven," we pray for at least three things. First, we ask to accept God's will. Second, we pray to approve God's will. Third, we pray to do God's will.

Prayer is the nearest approach to God and the highest enjoyment of Him that we are capable of in this life.
WILLIAM LAW

First we pray to accept God's will

God's will is done – always and everywhere. To try to live outside God's will is impossible. His will permeates all existence. In one sense, to oppose God's will is futile. We cannot break God's will – in the sense of preventing him from doing what he decides to do. We can only be broken in the attempt.

An ancient pagan king of Babylon, Nebuchadnezzar, found out about God's unbreakable will the hard way. One day he decided to take credit for his kingdom glory. As he walked the palace walls and surveyed Babylon and all its splendors – perhaps while looking at the hanging gardens, he boasted;

Daniel 4:30

Is not this the great Babylon I have built as the royal residence,
by my mighty power and for the glory of my majesty?

For this pride, Nebuchadnezzar was stripped of his throne and made to crawl on all fours until his hair looked like eagle's feathers and his claws like bird's claws. When he finally woke up to his folly, the first thing he proclaimed throughout his kingdom was that nothing and no one could stop God from doing what he would please to do:

Daniel 4:34-35

His dominion is an eternal dominion;
his kingdom endures from generation to generation.
All the peoples of the earth are regarded as nothing.
He does as he pleases with the powers of heaven
and the peoples of the earth. No one can hold back his hand
or say to him: "What have you done?"

Therefore, when we pray "your will be done," we affirm that God's rule and reign extends everywhere. We accept the limitation of our freedom when we pray, "your will be done." Only God is absolutely free and undetermined.

Psalm 115:3

Our God is in heaven;
he does whatever pleases him.

Everything in heaven and earth is created. God alone is creator. Every creature is dependent on the creation. He stands above the creation in his self determination and freedom. Our freedom is limited by our nature, our environment, and by God's plan and purposes.

Therefore, when we pray "your will be done," we worship God and ensure that all of our plans and purposes begin and end with "Deo Volenti," which means "God willing."

Second, we ask to approve God's will

When we accept God's will we do not just resign ourselves to it. God's will is not fate. His will is a living expression of his being and reveals his wisdom, justice, and truth. Once we get to know God's will and accept it, we soon learn to approve it:

Romans 12:2, 3

Do not conform any longer to the pattern of this world, but be transformed by the renewing of your mind. ***Then you will be able to test and approve what God's will is*** *– his good, pleasing and perfect will.*

Approving God's will is not always easy. Consider how the biblical character Job interprets God's will. Catastrophe strikes Job from all sides. He loses his property to looters, his animals to fire, and his children to a freak storm. What Job says reveals that he accepts and approves God's will:

Job 1:20-22

At this, Job got up and tore his robe and shaved his head. Then he fell to the ground in worship and said: "Naked I came from my mother's womb, and naked I will depart. The LORD gave and the LORD has taken away;

may the name of the LORD be praised." In all this, Job did not sin by charging God with wrongdoing.

This is not resignation. Job does not believe in fate. He knows that God's will is over every event of his life. He knows that God is not capricious or malicious, in spite of how circumstances appear. He believes that God has a higher purpose, even if Job cannot discern it.

Prayer is not conquering God's reluctance, but taking hold of God's willingness.
PHILLIPS BROOKS

Nor does Job believe he is being punished for his sins. He lives by grace and not by karma. When his 'friends' insist that he is getting what he deserves, Job maintains that God is not judging him as an offender, but is testing him as his child. To that end he refuses to characterize God as a heartless judge. This is the main theme of Job. He knows that Satan's tempting is God's testing.

This is important. When we pray, "your will be done" we are asking to understand and approve God's will – especially in the hard times.

The best example of accepting and approving of God's will is Jesus Christ himself. In his final days on earth, Jesus is in the garden of Gethsemane. He knows what agony is in store for him at the cross. He knows that he will be cruelly murdered. He already feels the burden of mankind's sin. In this terrible moment, Jesus does not just wrestle with fate. In prayer, he struggles with, and within, the will of God:

Then he said to them, "My soul is overwhelmed with sorrow to the point of death. Stay here and keep watch with me." Going a little farther, he fell with his face to the ground and prayed, "My Father, if it is possible, may this cup be taken from me. Yet not as I will, but as you will."

Matthew 26:38, 39

Jesus' sorrow is real, and his pain is intense, yet he realizes that his heavenly father permits his suffering for the highest of purposes – the salvation of a universe!

In the same way, the key to our growth in grace is to pray to approve of God's will for our lives:

I cry out to God, who fulfills his purpose for me.

Psalm 57:2

In believing prayer, we learn to connect our present troubles to the good and perfect will of God. We refuse to believe that chance rules our lives. We withstand the temptation to imagine that God is capricious or malicious. We know he has a higher purpose and that he is not dealing with us as our sins deserve. Listen to what Peter the apostle says about God's higher purposes:

Dear friends, do not be surprised at the painful trial you are suffering, as though something strange were happening to you. But rejoice that you participate in the sufferings of Christ, so that you may be overjoyed when his glory is revealed. If you are insulted because of the name of Christ, you are blessed, for the Spirit of glory and of God rests on you. So then, those who suffer according to God's will should commit themselves to their faithful Creator and continue to do good.

1Peter 4:12-14,19

As we bring our troubles to Jesus in prayer – asking his will to be done – we approve the will of our Father in heaven. We see our sufferings in the greater reality of his good, acceptable, and perfect will. In prayer we "turn crisis to Christ." Our heart becomes tuned to his heart and we sing the song of grace.

This is good news when it comes to prayer! Once we learn to accept and approve of God's will, we are able to pray with great effect and assurance. When we ask according to God's will, our will is tuned and in harmony with his will. We not only know God's will from the Bible, we have learned to approve his will from our spiritual growth and experience. Jesus calls this harmony with God's will "abiding":

John 15:5,7,8

> *I am the vine; you are the branches...If you* ***abide in me*** *and my words remain in you,* **ask whatever you wish, and it will be given you.** *This is to my Father's glory, that you bear much fruit, showing yourselves to be my disciples.*

Those who abide in Jesus learn to pray according to God's will, and have an inner assurance that their prayers are answered.

Third, we pray to do God's will on earth as in heaven

God's will is perfect. His will is unchangeable but is living and alive as God is. In order to make his will clear, God has given us commands as a rule and guide for life. He requires our obedience to his laws.

Once again, heaven is our example. The chief joy of the angels is to obey God's commands. In fact, we have no biblical examples of angels acting independently of Gods' commands:

Psalm 103:19-21

> *The Lord has established his throne in heaven, and his Kingdom rules over all. Praise the Lord, you his angels, you mighty ones who do his bidding and obey his word. Praise the Lord, all his heavenly hosts, you his servants who do his will.*

For us to pray and do God's will "as it is in heaven," we are not to obey God grudgingly, but to rejoice in obeying God.

God's commands are more than rules. Rules are simply legal boundaries. They are impersonal. Consider sporting events. The referee who executes the rules does not have to feel passionate about them. God's commands, in contrast, are not just rules. They express his holy character. They express his identity. God is not a disinterested referee who just makes sure the game is kept "in hand." He is passionate about his laws and for them to be kept – from the heart.

God's will includes a passion for justice. His will includes grief and sorrow for victims of injustice. To do God's will in its fullest sense, is more than mere obedience. True obedience includes sharing his passion for justice and his compassion for victims of injustice. God is internally committed to justice. In fact, justice is an attribute of God. His laws are supremely just. He appoints those who have authority in family, society and church to maintain justice and stop oppression.

Cruelty and injustice happen every day in every city. Women and children are molested. Many are physically abused – in their own homes. Innocent parties are left in ruins after ugly divorce battles. New immigrants are subject to prejudice and given demeaning work. The mentally ill are sent out of crowded hospitals and are left to fend for themselves on the streets. From their deepest heart, each victim cries questions of anguish, "Is my suffering God's will? Does God care? Is there justice? Will God rescue me from my oppressor?"

When we ask to do God's will, we commit to listen to struggle with these kinds of questions. We ask to know and to share God's passion for justice and his grief at injustice. We pray to hear the cries of the victim and ask to be willing to be the answer. Our prayer for God's will, therefore, is effective only if we share God's love of justice and hatred of oppression exploitation and violence.

Our prayers turn to deeds

It is not enough to just know God's will, or to pray for God's will to be done, we need grace and courage to obey and carry it out. The rubber has to hit the road. This is the "earth" where Jesus' will is to be done.

When we pray, "your will be done," we are committing to doing God's will. Facing the enormous social problems in our cities today, we do not say, "What has this got to do with me? This is the government's job." We cannot say, "This is not my problem. This is part of the wickedness of the world. I am separate from that. I have to protect and preserve my righteousness." Instead we pray, "Your will be done in me and through me." We pray for wisdom and courage to get involved with our city. God gives us wisdom. He will raise up leaders and servants to do his will.

In a *Showers for the Shelterless* program, we partner with others in our community to serve the homeless and mentally ill. We provide a gourmet coffee, breakfast and newspaper for our homeless. We visit and get to know them. We provide a "valet service" for their carts and dogs. The homeless won't come in if their belongings are unattended.

At a local housing project, we have worked with *More Than a Roof* to bring the gospel and community development to the tenants who live there. With *Genesis Vancouver,* a ministry to sexually exploited women and their children, we pray for and seek to serve the sexually exploited – to deliver them not only from pimps and "Johns" but also from a culture that exploits us all. We partner and pray for Genesis Vancouver to provide safe houses and day programs for the sexually exploited and their children.

There is a connection between our praying for justice and justice coming to pass. Speaking to Israel while exiled in Babylon, Jeremiah reminds his people to seek justice for their city.

> ***Seek the peace and prosperity of the city*** *to which I carried you in exile.* ***Pray to the Lord for it,*** *because if it prospers, you too will prosper...For I know the plans I have for you, declares the Lord, plans to prosper you and not to harm you, plans to give you hope and a future.* ***Then you will call upon me and I will listen to you.***

Jeremiah 29:7,11,12

Notice how prayer for the city is commanded. Notice how God promises he will answer with urban peace and prosperity.

Another striking passage is found in Isaiah 58. As in Jeremiah, there is a connection between our prayers for urban renewal and God's promise to hear this prayer. However, something crucial is added. God's answer to our prayer is that he sends us into the city to be his agents of transformation. He will rebuild the city. He will do it through those who pray. We become the answer to our own prayer!

Isaiah 58:6-12

Is this not the kind of fasting that I have chosen: to loose the chains of injustice and untie the cords of the yoke, to set the oppressed free and break every yoke? Is it not to share your food with the hungry and to provide the poor wanderer with shelter... Then your light will break forth like the dawn and your healing will quickly appear; then your righteousness will go before you and the glory of the Lord will be your rear guard. ***Then you will call and the Lord will answer; you will cry for help and he will say Here am I....Your people will rebuild the ancient ruins and will raise up the age old foundations; you will be called Repairer of Broken Walls, Restorer of Streets with Dwellings.***

> *God has instituted prayer so as to confer upon his creatures that dignity of being causes.*
> BLAISE PASCAL

The implication is clear. As God's people we are to pray for his will to be done on earth. We are to become deeply engaged with the needs of our city. God will answer our prayer as we do so. He will rescue the needy and establish safe neighborhoods. The way God renews the city is by sending his people to carry out this mandate. This is how his will is done on earth as it is in heaven.

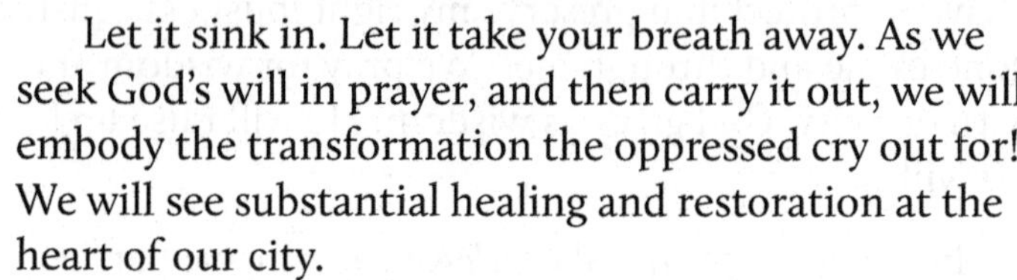

Let it sink in. Let it take your breath away. As we seek God's will in prayer, and then carry it out, we will embody the transformation the oppressed cry out for! We will see substantial healing and restoration at the heart of our city.

What a marvelous encouragement to prayer!

DAY 4

DAY 4

Prayerful Pondering

Questions for Reflection

* Where are you struggling with accepting and approving God's will in your life currently? Where do you need Jesus to settle your heart to his will? How does it make you feel knowing Jesus also struggled and suffered with and within the will of God?

* Who is your neighbour, practically speaking? How is God asking you to love them?

Summary of Key Idea(s)

What key thought(s) do you want to remember or revisit?

Prayer Prompts: *Use these points to guide your prayers. Try writing out your prayers.*

When we pray "Your will be done on earth as it is in heaven":

* We surrender and ask for our will to be in harmony with, and to do God's will.
* We bring our joys and troubles to Jesus in prayer, asking him to settle our hearts to his will. We ask to see our sufferings in the greater reality of his good and perfect will.
* We pray to hear the cry of the victim. We pray for passion for justice, for compassion and rehabilitation of both the victims and offenders of injustice.
* We ask to be willing to be the answer, to have wisdom and courage to obey and carry out his will on earth, and to get involved in the needs of our city.

Prayer Practice

Try praying through the newspaper one day this week. Ask God to show you his heart and his perspective for the people, places and problems that are in your city and world. Pray for God's will to be done.

DAY 4

Prayer Practice:
Preparing for a Daily Pattern for Prayer

Overview

Throughout this book, we will lead you through a pattern and sequence for prayer that focuses on one priority from Jesus' prayer each day. Today you will apply the pattern to "your will be done on earth as it is in heaven."

Pattern for Prayer ► *Applied to "Your will be done"*

1 *Priority & Promise*

Praise God for his promises & priorities

Start by focusing on the priority **UPWARD to God.** Allow the Holy Spirit to guide you through the priority for the day.

Praise Jesus for the priority. Meditate on **what it means,** what it reveals about God, about Jesus' passion and purpose.

* *Meditate on God's will for mercy and justice. Where you are weak, receive his new mercy and fresh courage to surrender. Thank Jesus for satisfying God's will.*

2 *Passions*

Pray God's promises & priorities into **your own heart**

Next pray the priority **INWARD into your heart.** Talk with God about your present heart state, allowing him to thoroughly examine and encourage you.

Ask Jesus to **transform your heart** and life to be more like his.

* *As you ponder God's will, allow the Holy Spirit to show you where you are growing in obedience. Thank him for growth. Confess and surrender your selfish ways.*
* *Pray for an obedient, merciful, and compassionate heart. Pray for a growing desire for justice, righteousness, and mercy.*

3 *People*

Pray God's promises as a **blessing to others**

Now pray **OUTWARD for others to experience more of God**'s promises.

Pray for **people,** your loved ones, other individuals, ministries, your church, city, and the world.

* *Think of people God has placed in your life as neighbours – work, family, friends, community. Pray for God's mercy on them. Ask for opportunities to practically extend mercy to them.*

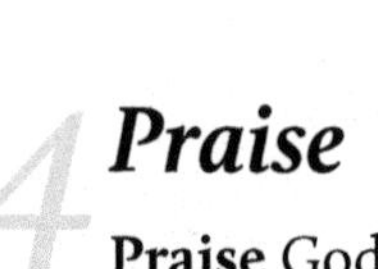

4 *Praise*

Praise God for all his blessings

End by **praising God** for his blessings and answers to prayer.

Recall how God has been present. Remember to **thank** him.

* *Praise God for new mercies you have experienced. Thank him for answers, blessings, or insights he reveals to you in your prayers.*

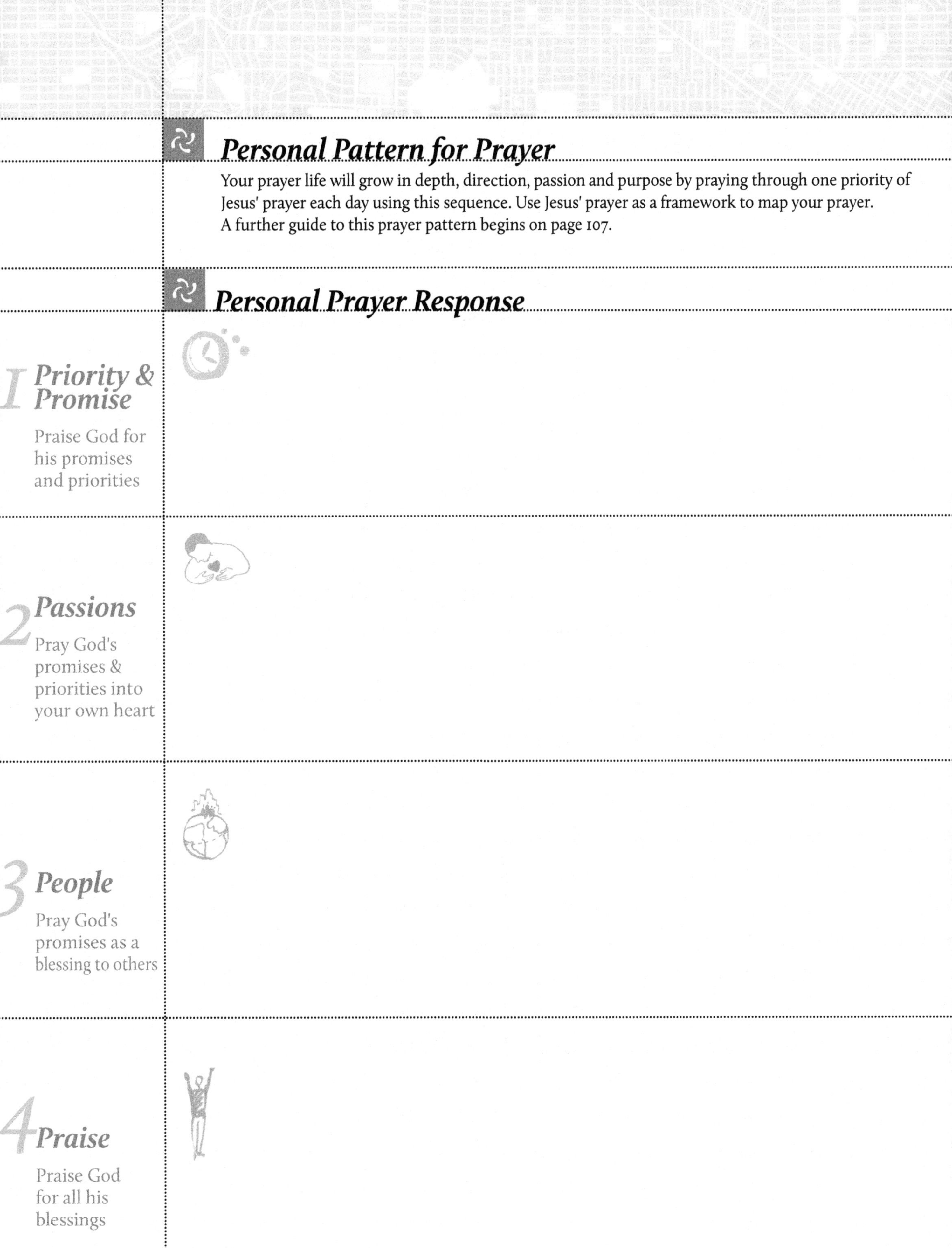

Personal Pattern for Prayer

Your prayer life will grow in depth, direction, passion and purpose by praying through one priority of Jesus' prayer each day using this sequence. Use Jesus' prayer as a framework to map your prayer. A further guide to this prayer pattern begins on page 107.

Personal Prayer Response

1 *Priority & Promise*

Praise God for his promises and priorities

2 *Passions*

Pray God's promises & priorities into your own heart

3 *People*

Pray God's promises as a blessing to others

4 *Praise*

Praise God for all his blessings

GIVE US THIS DAY

OUR DAILY BREAD

DAY 1 2 3 4 **5** 6 7

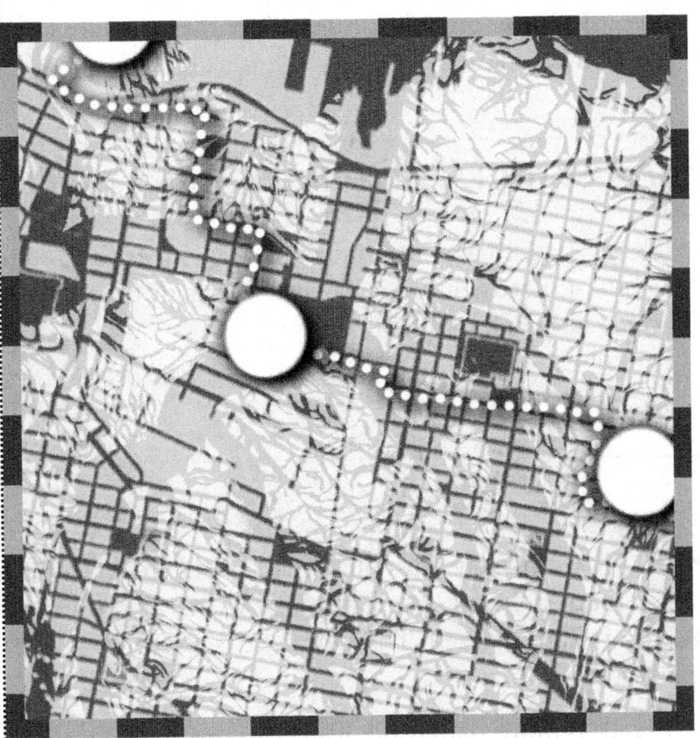

Earthly riches are full of poverty.

AUGUSTINE

I experienced today the most exquisite pleasure I ever had in my life.
I was able to breathe freely for about five minutes.

A YOUNG INVALID

Life cannot be satisfied when it is lived out as a consuming entity.

RAVI ZECHARIAS

DAY 5

GIVE US THIS DAY

Our Daily Bread

Today's Priority

* We give God heartfelt thanks for his abundant care.
* We ask to be content with what we have and confess our attachments to property and possessions.
* We ask God to provide for us and for our neighbors with a sufficient portion of life's necessities.

Purpose and Outcome of this Prayer

* As we ask each day, each morning, each meal, for God to provide our basic needs, our life will be increasingly characterized by thankfulness, generosity, and simplicity.

"Give us this day our daily bread." Jesus covers a lot of ground with this request. In these seven simple words all our prayers for earthly concerns are summarized. This sentence is a sermon with rich and varied applications.

Matthew 4:4

John 6:35

"Bread" is more than food. Jesus teaches a great deal about bread and encourages us to take this term more than literally. Bread is flour and yeast. Bread also refers to the Word of God. "Man does not live by bread alone but by every word that proceeds from the mouth of God." Bread refers to the enjoyment of the gospel. "I have bread to eat that you do not know." Bread also refers to faith in him. "I am the bread of life." "Bread" is a symbol or metaphor for all of life's necessities. When we ask for daily bread we can ask for good weather, good government, and good health. We pray for the environment.

Farmers understand this expanded concept of bread. When a farmer grows wheat for bread he checks government quotas, consults his almanac about the weather, analyzes the soil, and checks out the price of wheat on the world market. In the world of wheat, government, environment, climate, and economy are inseparable from bread.

In most places around the world political and social peace are needed for there to be sufficient bread. Times of war are often times of scarcity and famine. When government agents divert or commandeer donated grain, people starve. When we pray for daily bread it is implied that we ask for just government for ourselves and others.

Good health is important for us to enjoy our daily bread. Many cannot enjoy their food or even keep it down because of some ravaging cancer or wasting disease. Robbie Burns penned a prayer:

Some ha' meat that canna' eat.
Some na' ha' meat that want it.
We ha' meat, and we ca' eat
Sa the Lord be thanked.

Good health is a blessing given by God. Prayers for health and healing fit with our prayer for daily bread.

When we pray for daily bread, our request has a specific meaning as well as a comprehensive application. When we ask for bread, we are asking for all of life's necessities as well as the peace and health to enjoy them.

Asking for daily bread slowly changes our entire outlook on life

As we faithfully and intelligently pray this amazing prayer we not only receive what we ask for – bread – we also discover that Jesus is transforming our hearts and minds in the act of prayer. First, he is teaching us trust and thankfulness. Second, he is building generosity and kindness. Third, Jesus is developing our contentment and simplicity of life. We become what we pray.

1. As we pray this prayer we learn trust and thankfulness

As we humbly ask, "Give us this day our daily bread," we acknowledge our dependence on God for everything that we have. All good things come from God – given as a gift from his hand. "Praise God from whom all blessings flow."

When we pretend self-sufficiency or credit our own labor and industry for the prosperity we enjoy, we are denying that life is a gift.

Jesus is not a laissez-faire capitalist. He does not leave our well being to economic laws and forces. He does not view people as means of production, nor does he measure worth by productivity.

It is an illusion to credit ourselves for the good things we enjoy. If someone is able to provide jobs for others – it is by God's grace. God gives family, government, health, and opportunity to do well in these matters. In Canada, a wealthy person puts in a long day to make a good living. In Calcutta, a rickshaw driver works day and night to make a few rupees. If a person is poor, it may not have anything to do with how industrious he is. He or she may not have the opportunity to make a good living.

When we pray for bread, "we lift up empty hands." Our hands are empty of our own enterprise and industry. We depend on God to fill all our needs from his own bounty and kindness. Asking for daily bread involves turning from self-reliance and asking for a heart that relies on God.

Trust in God's provision is enriched with thankfulness of heart

The habit of asking implies a response of thanksgiving. There is no greater proof of Jesus' work in our hearts than genuine thankfulness.

Thanksgiving is an antidote to greed and to envy. It is a speed bump on our restless road of acquisition. Thanksgiving cuts envy at the seed stage – before it sprouts. A widespread practice of thanksgiving will slow down greed and envy in any culture. Some prayer barely veils our selfish attempt:

One man asked God, "How much is a million years to you?"
"Only a second," replied God.
The man then asked, "How much is a million dollars to you?"
"Only a penny," replied God.
"Could you give me one of your pennies God?"
"Just give me a second."

When we give thanks we take our eyes off what we do not have. God grows larger in our faith. The sacrificial gift of Jesus becomes more than sufficient for our troubles. When we take a plane to 35,000 feet – we look down and get a new perspective on life. Everything looks smaller. In the same way, in thankful prayer we rise above daily problems. Our needs diminish in size and significance. In prayer we see the abundance of God and the fullness of life he has given us. We can't help but feel deeply thankful. It is amazing how discontent with the bills, mortgage, and expenses of life disappears when we give thanks for the abundance on our table each day.

My wife Caron and I once were involved with a drug and alcohol recovery program. The participants, mostly teenagers, were required to write a "grat-list" every day. Before going to bed each one would take time to ponder and write out a list, often a long one, of all they were grateful for. Over the months we watched a gradual transformation take place in many of the kids. In an amazing way they moved from morbid self-centeredness to self-respect and appreciation for others. Their gratitude for daily blessings turned to gratefulness for life.

Achieving thankfulness is at the heart of Jesus' plan for his people.

Nehemiah 12:27,31

When the Israelites returned from the Babylonian captivity and rebuilt the city walls, they sought out the priestly workers "to celebrate joyfully the dedication with songs of thanksgiving." The leaders also "assigned two large choirs to give thanks."

1Thess. 5:18

Paul tells the church to "give thanks in all circumstances." To the believers at Philippi Paul explains how thankfulness cures worry:

Philippians 4:6,7

Do not be anxious about anything, but in everything, by prayer and petition, ***with thankssgiving,*** *present your requests to God. And the peace of God, which transcends all understanding, will guard your hearts and your minds in Christ Jesus.*

Colossians 1:10-12

Prayer awakens the power of the risen Christ in us. As we pray we move from anxiety and restlessness about possessions to a spirit of "joyfully giving thanks." When we start our day, or begin a meal with simple thankfulness, we are cultivating an attitude of contentment and inner joy.

2. As we pray we learn kindness and generosity

We do not ask "Give *me* this day *my* daily bread." We pray "give *us* this day *our* daily bread." This prayer is prayed in community. This is a prayer for others as much as it is a prayer for oneself. It is a call to kindness and compassion.

As we ask for daily bread, we are praying for the children of God all over the world. The church is a believer's forever-family. For a Christian to imagine a brother or sister living in poverty, nakedness, and hunger is impossible:

> *If anyone has material possessions and sees his brother in need but has no pity on him, how can the love of God be in him? No one can say they love God, whom they cannot see, if they do not love their brother whom they do see.*

1John 4:20

We also pray for our friends, neighbors, family– indeed our country and whole world – to have daily bread. All people are made in God's image and are worthy of all care, kindness, and love. We love our neighbor in prayer. We love our neighbor in deeds.

Jesus' parable of the Good Samaritan teaches us never to discriminate when it comes to compassion and kindness. The wounded and naked person on the roadside is Jewish. The Jews were sworn enemies of the Samaritans. While religious types, the priest, and the Levite, walk by the other side of the road, the Samaritan bandages and feeds his enemy. This foreigner's love for God is evidenced in his compassion.

Luke 10:25-37

When we pray this prayer we are asking for a generous spirit

When we ask for daily bread, we ask for the ability and willingness to give an increasing portion of what we have to others in need. Jesus says, "Freely you have received. Freely give." No matter how much we make or own, we ask to be content with a modest portion. We pray for courage and integrity to give sacrificially to Christ's mission and to those in need. Christian giving is sacrificial because it is modeled on the sacrifice of Jesus:

Matthew 10:8

> *For you know the grace of our Lord Jesus Christ, that though he was rich, yet for your sakes he became poor, so that you through his poverty might become rich.*

2 Corinthians 8:9

Jesus said, "It is more blessed to give than to receive." Giving to others in need is a powerful antidote to greed and covetousness.

Acts 20:35

There is nothing wrong with giving to ourselves. In fact it would be wrong not to. Jesus says, "Love your neighbor as yourself." This means we should love and care for ourselves as well as for our neighbor.

Life is meant to be lived in balance. Our life is a "mini Trinity" of relationships – God, others, and self. A balanced person divides and balances his or her time, energy, and resources on God first, others second, and self third.

However, anything near this balance is rare. The average North American gives two per cent to four per cent of his or her net income to others. This includes Christians. On average, each of us is spending more than 95 per cent of life's income on ourselves. No matter how we slice it, this is not a life of balance. There is too little left for God and others.

This lack of balance leads to ill health and a poor state of mind. We can trace a good deal of spiritual unhappiness and discontent to a preoccupation with self. As we follow Jesus in day-by-day prayer for bread, God will lead us to a life of kindness and generosity - to a life of balance.

3. We learn contentment and simplicity from this prayer

When we ask God for "this day's" bread, we are called to seek God's provision one day at a time. We leave tomorrow to him. We ask God to forgive our anxiety and restless striving to grasp tomorrow before it comes.

"Oh, Earth, you're too wonderful for anyone to realize you!...Do any human beings ever realize life while they live it - every, every moment?" *Emily in* Our Town *by* THORTON WILDER

This is the lesson of the manna.

The children of Israel are led through a wilderness for forty years. God provides them daily bread - called manna. Each day the Israelites go out and gather this manna from the ground - which they cook, bake, or boil. It contains everything they need in the way of nourishment.

However, this manna only lasts that day. It is useless to gather more than enough for one day. It simply rots overnight.

God provides his children a lesson of daily trust in this. He teaches the Israelites to look to him one day at a time to give them all they need. When we ask "this day" for bread we commit to a day-by-day reliance on him.

In the Sermon on the Mount, Jesus reinforces this call to live life a day at a time - not to fret about what God will bring tomorrow. He uses birds and flowers to teach us faith and contentment:

Matthew 6:25-29,33-34

Therefore I tell you, do not worry about your life, what you will eat or drink; or about your body, what you will wear ... Look at the birds of the air; they do not sow or reap or store away in barns, and yet your heavenly Father feeds them. Are you not much more valuable than they? Who of you by worrying can add a single hour to his life?

And why do you worry about clothes? See how the lilies of the field grow. They do not labor or spin. Yet I tell you that not even Solomon in all his splendor was dressed like one of these. But seek first his kingdom and his righteousness, and all these things will be given to you as well. ***Therefore do not worry about tomorrow, for tomorrow will worry about itself. Each day has enough trouble of its own.***

Each time I pray this prayer for daily bread, I take time to thank God for the various kinds of "daily bread" I enjoy. I ask God to help me to trust him one day at a time. I ask him to forgive and still my restless need to store up for tomorrow.

In this word "daily" we put a priority on contentment

We ask, "Give us this day our *daily bread.*" We ask for one day's bread. A sufficient but modest quantity is implied. We ask for a portion of life's blessings that is enough for this day. We do not ask for too little - so that we could not pay our bills, provide for our dependents, and help those in need. Yet, we ask for bread, not for a life of luxury and indulgence.

When we ask for daily bread, we leave it in God's hands to decide how much or how little is right for us. He can take us through times of want and scarcity. He can protect us through times of abundance, as the apostle Paul testified:

I know what it is to be in need, and I know what it is to have plenty.
I have learned the secret of being content in any and every situation,
whether well fed or hungry, whether living in plenty or in want.

Philippians 4:11

We may have savings accounts, insurance, and retirement plans, but we dare not trust in them for security. How easily these "storehouses" become a substitute for daily reliance upon God! If we are not careful, our happiness becomes attached to our wealth. Devotion to property becomes a substitute for relationship with God. Jesus tells us a simple and powerful parable about this "storehouse" problem:

Then Jesus said to them, "Watch out! Be on your guard against all kinds of greed; a man's life does not consist in the abundance of his possessions."

And he told them this parable: "The ground of a certain rich man produced a good crop. He thought to himself, 'What shall I do? I have no place to store my crops.'

"Then he said, 'This is what I'll do. I will tear down my barns and build bigger ones, and there I will store all my grain and my goods. And I'll say to myself, "You have plenty of good things laid up for many years. Take life easy; eat, drink and be merry."

"But God said to him, 'You fool! This very night your life will be demanded from you. Then who will get what you have prepared for yourself?'

"This is how it will be with anyone who stores up things for himself but is not rich toward God."

Luke 12:14-21

God knows what each of his children can handle. God knows what we need. He knows how much we need. He has a perfect plan for us. Poverty or riches is not the issue - contentment is.

Asking for "bread" encourages a life of simplicity

Bread is wonderful. Walk into any bakery early in the morning and you know what I mean. The aroma stirs every hungry cell. Yet bread is the simplest of foods. In this petition we ask to live with increasing simplicity.

> *"There is no gift his hand bestows but cost his heart a groan."*
> ANONYMOUS

We confess our tendency to live for, to obsess over, and to be completely attached to our property and possessions. Life becomes crowded with concerns about "bread."

Simplicity is difficult for us. Most often, spending increases with income. When we sell a house at a good profit; inherit some money, or receive a raise or bonus, without thinking, we immediately plan how to spend or save it. We make our lives more cluttered than before!

In our aptly named "consumer culture," this habit of increased acquisition seems obvious and right. In contrast, Jesus' call to simplicity seems quaint or absurd. However, following Jesus and praying this prayer has radical consequences. What once seemed obvious now becomes absurd. What was absurd becomes obvious. Simplicity becomes a beautiful thing. Luxury and self-indulgence become ugly.

Prayerful Pondering

Questions for Reflection

* What are you thankful for today?

* Where are you struggling with anxiety or self-reliance? Are your prayers more characterized by worry or thanksgiving?

* How much are your heart and life characterized by contentment? In what ways do you struggle with self-indulgence, desire for accumulating more, or greed? What are your challenges in living simply?

* How much of your time/talent/treasure are you spending on yourself? On others? On God? How might God be calling you to adjust the balance?

Summary of Key Idea(s) *What key thought(s) do you want to remember or revisit?*

Prayer Prompts: *Use these points to guide your prayers. Try writing out your prayers.*

When we pray for "our daily bread":

* We thank God for all that we have, recognizing it all as a grace from him. We ask for a spirit of thankfulness, contentment with what we have, simplicity in our living, and generosity with what he has given us.
* We confess our anxieties and our self-sufficiency. We ask for a heart that trusts and relies on God's abundance. We surrender our restless need to store up for tomorrow.
* We pray for our country and world to have daily bread. We ask for good government, wisdom for public leaders and policy makers, peace and health to enjoy life's necessities.

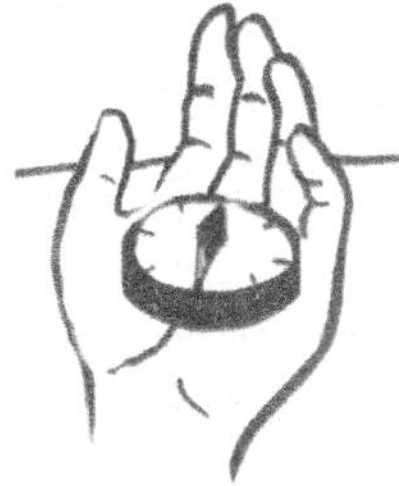

Prayer Practice

Try focusing your prayers this week on thanksgiving and praise. Write a short list of a few things for which you are grateful in your own life and in your city.

DAY 5

Prayer Practice:
Preparing for a Daily Pattern for Prayer

Overview

Throughout this book, we will lead you through a pattern and sequence for prayer that focuses on one priority from Jesus' prayer each day. Today you will apply the pattern to "give us this day our daily bread."

Pattern for Prayer → Applied to *"Give us our daily bread"*

1 **Priority & Promise**

Praise God for his promises & priorities

Start by focusing on the priority **UPWARD to God.** Allow the Holy Spirit to guide you through the priority for the day.

Praise Jesus for the priority. Meditate on **what it means,** what it reveals about God, about Jesus' passion and purpose.

* *Meditate on the sufficiency of God and his trustworthiness to provide for our every need. Thank him for the many daily blessings in your life. Feed on Jesus as the Bread of Life.*

2 **Passions**

Pray God's promises & priorities into **your own heart**

Next pray the priority **INWARD into your heart.** Talk with God about your present heart state, allowing him to thoroughly examine and encourage you.

Ask Jesus to **transform your heart** and life to be more like his.

* *Thank God for any growing evidence or desire you see for simplicity, contentment and generosity in your heart and life.*
* *Ask the Holy Spirit to reveal anything you may need to confess – self-reliance, greed, attachment to wealth and possessions, worry for tomorrow. Ask for an increasing trust and reliance on Christ.*

3 **People**

Pray God's promises as a **blessing to others**

Now pray **OUTWARD for others to experience more of God**'s promises.

Pray for **people,** your loved ones, other individuals, ministries, your church, city, and the world.

* *Pray for any needs (financial, health, etc.) of which you are aware for your neighbours, church, and city.*
* *Pray for your city and world to have daily bread. Pray for the economy, good government and peace. Pray for your (municipal, provincial, federal) politicians.*
* *Pray for your church and God's people to grow in generosity.*

4 **Praise**

Praise God for all his blessings

End by **praising God** for his blessings and answers to prayer.

Recall how God has been present. Remember to **thank** him.

* *Praise God for his abundant provision. Thank him for answers, blessings, or insights he reveals to you in your prayers.*

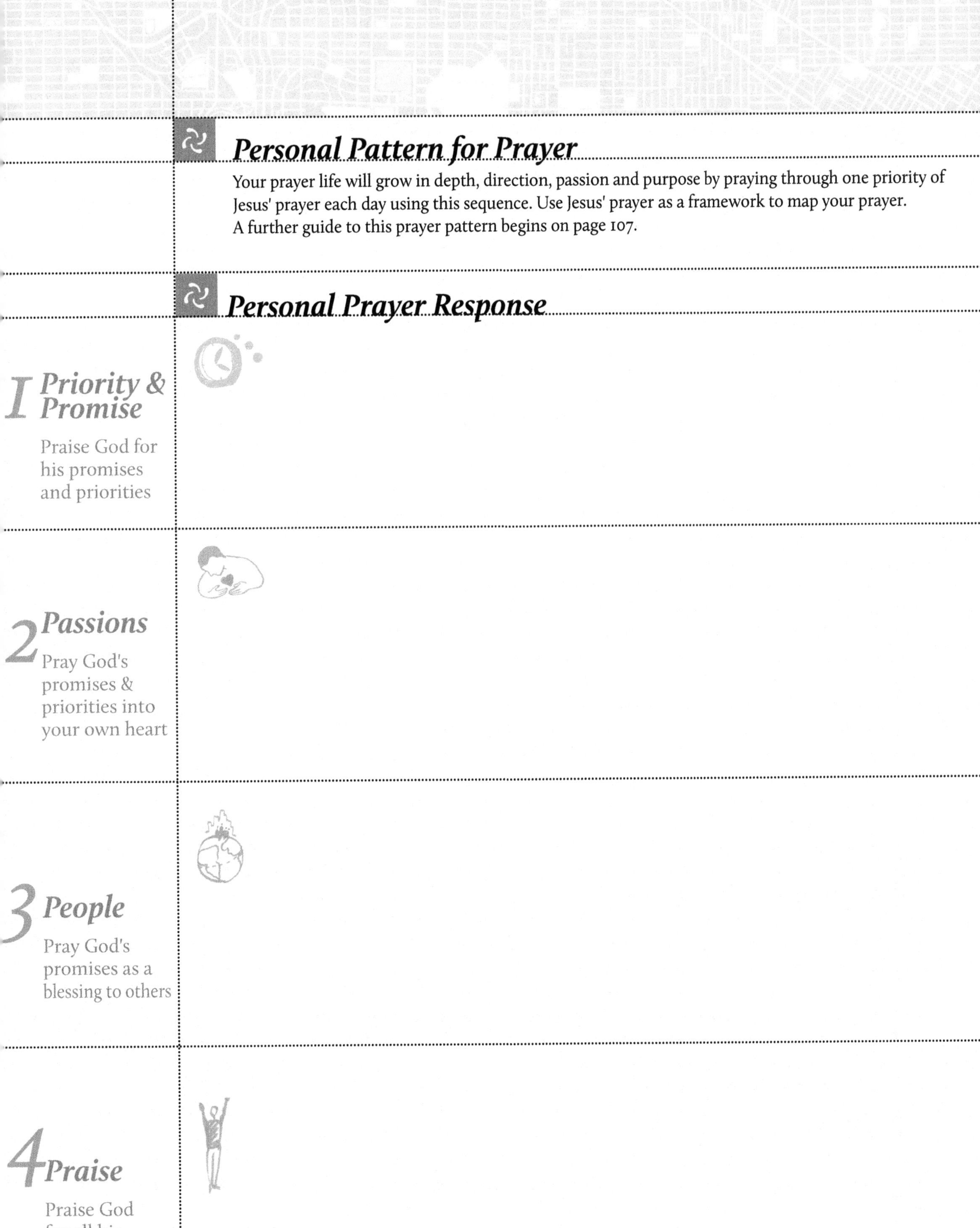

Personal Pattern for Prayer

Your prayer life will grow in depth, direction, passion and purpose by praying through one priority of Jesus' prayer each day using this sequence. Use Jesus' prayer as a framework to map your prayer. A further guide to this prayer pattern begins on page 107.

Personal Prayer Response

1 Priority & Promise

Praise God for his promises and priorities

2 Passions

Pray God's promises & priorities into your own heart

3 People

Pray God's promises as a blessing to others

4 Praise

Praise God for all his blessings

Forgive Us

OUR DEBTS AS WE FORGIVE OUR DEBTORS

DAY 1 2 3 4 5 **6** 7

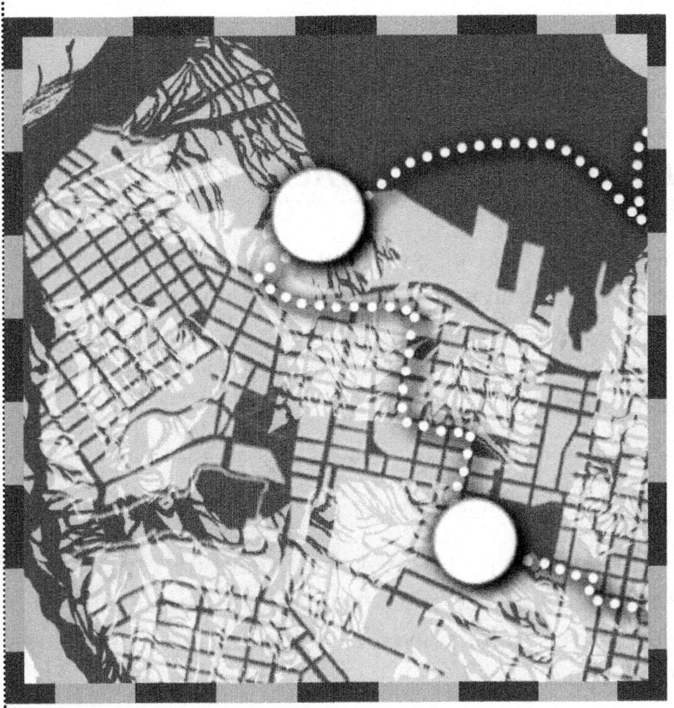

Criticism of others nails them to the past. Prayer for others releases them to the future.
Frank Laubach

We cannot be wrong with man and right with God.
"The Kneeling Christian"

DAY 6

Forgive Us

OUR DEBTS AS WE FORGIVE OUR DEBTORS

Today's Priority

* We focus on reconciliation through forgiveness. We receive reconciliation from God which flows into forgiveness for others.

Purpose and Outcome of this Prayer

* As we pray for forgiveness we enter into the amazing grace for which Jesus gave his life. When we ask for grace to forgive others we participate in the suffering and forgiveness of the cross. As we pray for reconciliation the spiritual entropy of this world is reversed – we experience healing and radical new beginnings.

It is curious that Jesus leaves this urgent necessity towards the end of his prayer. Why did he not start with forgiveness? The answer lies in the nature of Jesus' prayer. In his prayer, as in his life, Jesus puts God first. He teaches us to do the same.

Another reason Jesus leaves this request until the end of his prayer is so we know how to approach God and so we know what to ask forgiveness for.

As soon as you find a reason for evil, you no longer have evil. Evil has no meaning. By its very nature evil is irrational.
MIROSLAV VOLF

For example, the only way we can shoulder the responsibility of confessing our sin is to have a clear view of the Fatherhood of God. "Our Father" sets the relational context which permits a humble, courageous approach to God – faults and all. If we do not come to God as father, we will tend to approach him as a forbidding judge. We walk away feeling obligated to suffer for our faults. We feel burdened to pay God back with good deeds.

What we need to be forgiven of

We need to be forgiven for our sins. But, what is sin? There is no easy answer to this question. Seneca said, "Sin is complex and admits infinite variations." Dan Allender, a psychologist, writes:

> *It is impossible to make sense of evil. Evil is unexplainable. It does not make sense; it is non-being and non-sense.*

Sin concerns wrong behavior. You know the list – idolatry, murder, promiscuity, stealing, and lying. Yet we know sin goes deeper. It includes our thoughts and motives: hatred, envy, greed, malice, pride, and self-righteousness. Jesus said, "Whoever nurses anger against a brother has committed murder."

Matthew 5:22

Sin is more than isolated actions or thoughts. Sin is about relationships. When we sin we offend God, others, and self. All sin is deeply personal and relational.

Think about it. On a ***vertical level,*** when we sin against God it is more than breaking a rule. It is personal. If we choose another god to worship besides God Almighty, we subvert our relationship with him. We "cheat" on him. When we enjoy life's blessings without giving thanks, we edit God out of the picture. We deny God is our creator and provider. When we live out of our own industry and plans, we hurt our sonship relation to God. When we seek to achieve our own righteousness we plow around God as our redeemer – who gave his only son for our righteousness and forgiveness.

Sin is also personal on a ***horizontal level.*** When we intentionally injure someone physically or with our words, we damage our relationship with them. When we steal what belongs to someone or are greedy or envious of their well being, we undermine our bond with them. When someone is married and commits adultery, they betray wife, family, and many others.

Sin is serious. It wounds people and breaks relationships. The only way to restore these relationships is for Jesus to be wounded and broken for us.

Prayer is a labor above all labors since he who prays must wage a mighty warfare against the doubt and murmuring excited by the faintheartedness and unworthiness we feel within us.

LUTHER

The high price for our forgiveness

Forgiveness is free but it is not cheap. The highest price possible is paid that we might receive forgiveness as a free gift. Forgiveness is the reason for Jesus' life and the purpose of his sacrificial death on the cross.

After viewing Mel Gibson's *The Passion of the Christ*, many wondered why Jesus had to suffer so brutally. False accusations, hours of whipping, a wreath of thorns, spitting and mocking, hands being nailed to rough sawn wood, and the terrible cry, "My God, my God, why have you forsaken me?" All of Jesus' suffering is drawn out in painful, slow, and graphic detail. Is this overkill?

The answer is "No!" Everything about Jesus' sacrifice is needed and necessary – no more, no less. The brutality of the cross is a measure of the horror of human sin. The violence of the passion is proportional to the sum total of human violence against God and those made in his image. The alienation Jesus experiences when forsaken on the cross parallels the alienation of a world permeated by sin.

This is not overkill. Put all hatred, malice, envy, lust, deceit, betrayal – in all the wars, rapes, genocides, abuse, and oppression in humankind's sad history and you will understand the infinite price required and paid to remove our sin and provide forgiveness forever.

Yet, Jesus' death is not a tragedy. His suffering brings good news. He conquers sin and defeats death at the cross. His great suffering achieves reconciliation for every offender who comes to God for forgiveness of sin.

In fact, Jesus' suffering is sufficient for any crime, cruelty, or injustice you or anyone else has ever committed. This very day, all you have to do is humbly ask. When you confess your sins and trust in Jesus' completed work on the cross – you are completely washed clean of your sin. As you repeat this asking and trusting every day, you are renewed in forgiveness. An old saying captures this truth:

That Jesus died on the cross is history.
That Jesus died for sin is theology.
That Jesus died for my sin is Christianity.

Even as you read this, remember why Jesus died. Ask him to apply his sacrifice to you and to forgive your sins. Become the renewed person he died for you to be.

The challenge of receiving forgiveness

In our conscience we are aware of the seriousness of sin. We know that a high price and costly sacrifice must be paid to remove it. We need great assurances from God in order to find the humility and courage to confess our sins. We need the promises of God:

Isaiah 1:18

"Come now, let us reason together," says the LORD.
"Though your sins are like scarlet, they shall be as white as snow;
though they are red as crimson, they shall be like wool."

Psalm 103:12

As far as the east is from the west,
so far has he removed our
transgressions from us.

1 John 1:9

If we confess our sins, he is faithful and
just and will forgive us our sins and
purify us from all unrighteousness.

It takes grace to confess, and to receive forgiveness. We struggle with residual guilt and a deep sense of unworthiness. We rehearse our faults again and again. We wrestle with a desire to do penance and suffer for our sins.

What can we do about our reluctance to receive forgiveness? We must rehearse these great promises of Scripture. We remind ourselves that God forgets our sin once he forgives it.

Most important, we need to look long and hard at the sacrifice of Jesus. God not only promises to forgive and forget our sin, he achieves and guarantees forgiveness through Jesus and his perfect and complete sacrifice.

Forgiveness is as complete and finished as the perfect sacrifice of Jesus

These verses tell how Jesus is the only one who can remove the guilt and the power of sin:

Isaiah 53:6

We all, like sheep, have gone astray,
each of us has turned to his own way;
and ***the LORD has laid on him the iniquity of us all.***

Zech. 13:1

"On that day a fountain will be opened to the house of David
and the inhabitants of Jerusalem, ***to cleanse them from sin and impurity.***

1 John 2:1,2

If anybody does sin, we have one who speaks to the Father in our
defense—Jesus Christ, the Righteous One. ***He is the atoning sacrifice***
for our sins and not only for ours but also for the sins of the whole world.

To experience a deep sense of complete and perfect forgiveness we not only need to rehearse the promises of God – we need to study the sacrifice of Jesus on our behalf. The principle is this – don't dwell on your sin and guilt, but look steadily at Jesus. His sacrifice has infinite value to cancel your debt. Your sins are forever nailed to the cross.

Let us draw near to God with a sincere heart in full assurance of faith, having our hearts sprinkled to cleanse us from a guilty conscience and having our bodies washed with pure water.

Hebrews 10:22

The challenge and joy of learning to forgive others

When we ask for forgiveness it is "as we forgive our debtors." We confess our sin, and we extend this forgiveness to others as well. Receiving forgiveness is only half the picture.

Jesus takes a strong stand on forgiving others. He teaches that we are to extend forgiveness without exception:

For if you forgive men when they sin against you, your heavenly Father will also forgive you. But if you do not forgive men their sins, your Father will not forgive your sins.

Matthew 6:14

Jesus tells us to forgive without excuse for how often or how deep the offense:

When Peter came to Jesus and asked, "Lord, how many times shall I forgive my brother when he sins against me? Up to seven times?" Jesus answered, "I tell you, not seven times, but seventy-seven times."

Matthew 18:21

It may take time, but we are usually able to find grace to forgive when an apology is offered. What are we to do, however, when someone sins against us but does not acknowledge their debt?

Overlooking a fault is possible in the "misdemeanors" of life. A slighting, a rough word, minor neglect, or criticism – such wounds often heal in their own time. What are we to do, however, with the "felonies" of life? Consider victims of adultery or wrongful divorce. The agony of betrayal tears their heart apart. Others are defrauded in business and investments – and lose everything.
Who can heal their bitter disappointment? When someone is falsely accused and condemned – the shame and injustice seem unbearable. There are children who have been sexually or physically abused, often for years. In the midst of relentless pain – how do they forgive those who have hurt them?

Forgiveness and reconciliation seem like a distant or impossible dream. Yet, the victim can never be fully healed without forgiveness. The torn relationship will continue to bring pain. A bitter and unforgiving heart will only hurt the victim.

Jesus understands the danger of not forgiving others. There are at least three very good reasons for Jesus' strong stand on forgiving others.

One reason why we must forgive is by comparison. When it comes to the seriousness of the fault, the debt owed to us cannot compare with the debt we owe to God. Nor can the small sacrifice I pay to forgive someone compare with the price Jesus paid. It may cost a wound in order to forgive someone who has hurt me. God paid the ultimate price.

A second reason we must forgive is logic. When we ask for forgiveness we need to confess all of our sins. Perhaps the greatest sin any of us needs forgiveness for is an unforgiving heart. Over years Miroslav Volf struggled with hatred and a desire for revenge against the Serbian forces that ravaged his country of Croatia. He recounts how God taught him the important lesson about forgiving others:

> *We must not forget that there is an evil worse than the original crime. It consists of self-centered slothfulness of the mind, heart, and will that will not recognize one's own sinfulness, not pursue justice for the innocent, and not extend grace to the guilty.*

A third reason we forgive others is that not forgiving can kill our heart. "Unforgiveness is the poison I drink trying to kill you." An unforgiving heart breeds grudges and bitterness – eventually killing the capacity to love. When we deny our sin, or harbor an unforgiving heart, we rob ourselves of the joy and release of forgiveness. An unforgiving person can become incapable of loving others. Without forgiveness, friends come and go, but enemies accumulate.

When sin remains unforgiven, grudges resurface. Sin is a kind of toxic waste that lasts forever if not removed by forgiveness. There was a company that tried to drill a mile deep hole to bury toxic waste. After disposing the PCB's, they filled the hole with cement. A few years later poisonous water surfaced. PCB's contaminated the water which seeped upwards though cracks and crevices in the underground rock.

This is how sin works. You can repress or deny it, but it will always resurface and destroy relationships. One counselor said, "What you don't reconcile you recycle."

Take a church community. Churches thrive in the environment of forgiveness. A church that practices forgiveness experiences the deep rewards of reconciliation. Love that survives conflict and disagreement is always deeper and more meaningful than shallow and surface love. A church that survives divisions and attacks of sin will be stronger and more loving than before.

Without forgiveness, however, a church is in trouble. Unforgiven sin is like an inner volcano which can explode into a war of words – or worse. Once broken relations and wounded hearts are left to fester, gossip and resentment step in. Gossip is like a British Columbian forest fire in dry season. An exploding fir tree shoots embers up to two kilometers ahead! In a matter of days thousands of acres of forest are burning out of control. Towns and cities are forced to evacuate. When the fire is in full force, fire fighters' efforts are useless. They can only sit and pray for rain.

Gossip is like this forest fire. Unchecked, it leaps from heart to heart, mouth to mouth, until the whole church is ablaze. The only hope is concerted prayer as we wait for the cleansing rains of God's grace – as we ask for a spirit of contrition and confession.

When you pray this prayer, it is essential to examine if you have been gossiping.

God gives power and hope to forgive others

For those wounded without an apology there is hope. For those who have suffered violence, betrayal, or neglect of others, there is good news. You can take your wounds to Jesus – his wounds heal your wounds.

We lay our heavy burden on him. He is called "man of sorrows." He knows what it means to be a victim. *He died not only to remove our sins but also to heal our sicknesses and sorrows.* This is a profound realization for those tormented with the bitterness and sorrow that comes from the wounds of sin:

> *Surely he took up our infirmities and carried our sorrows,*
> *the punishment that brought us peace was upon him,*
> *and by his wounds we are healed.*

Isaiah 53:5

Jesus not only died to forgive us of our sins. He gave his life to heal us of every wound we have had to suffer in a sinful and violent world. This healing makes it possible for us to forgive others – from the heart.

Even while you are healing, you can also take your "enemy" to Jesus in prayer. Prayer is the first and most important step in restoring relationships with others:

> *I can no longer condemn or hate a brother for whom I pray, no matter how much trouble he causes me. ~Dietrich Bonhoeffer*

> *Last night when praying I suddenly realized that I had really forgiven someone I have been trying to forgive for over thirty years. ~CS Lewis*

After bringing your wounds to Jesus and after praying for the one who has hurt you – when your heart is ready and when it is safe to do so, Jesus encourages you to go to your offender to seek reconciliation. In justice and in love you are to pray for your "enemy" and to approach them in order to help them acknowledge their sin and move towards reconciliation.

> *If your brother sins against you, go and show him his fault, just between the two of you. If he listens to you, you have won your brother over.*

Matthew 18:15

This "intervention" requires wisdom and patience. We must ask for love and courage in order to be effective. Without love we are judgmental. Without courage we will stop short of the goal. We must also ask for God to open the door for the right opportunity. As he hears our prayers the hope for reconciliation becomes real.

A friend told me how they confronted their abusive father. It was many years after the fact, and the father was now infirm and elderly. With tears and apprehension, my friend simply asked, "Why Dad? Why?"

What did this offending father say to this hurting child? He broke down and cried. "Oh, I am so sorry for what I have done. Forgive me." What a glorious surprise for my friend! What a beginning for hope.

In my own case, after years of prayer for someone who had hurt me, I finally had the courage to speak to him. It took years for me to even acknowledge my hurt and their fault. Fear of rejection kept me from seeing the truth. I prayed about this. God gave me love and courage. One day we got together. God opened the door for meaningful conversation. It went wonderfully. The atmosphere was full of truth. In fact, after willingly acknowledging his fault, this person also confronted me about my resentment and arrogance. We both felt better afterwards. Something important had happened. We experienced reconciliation through forgiveness. Our relationship has been growing ever since.

Forgiveness results in relational reconciliation

Reconciliation is the key to lasting and growing relationships with others. I think of my marriage. Caron and I have been together for over thirty years and have raised five children, and we have a growing number of grandchildren. Through many bumps and bruises our love has continually grown through the years. The key is not compatibility or strength of character. The secret is reconciliation through forgiveness. Saying "Sorry" and "I forgive you" improves a marriage.

Parent-child relationships grow and deepen with an honest admission of failings – on both sides. No matter how weak our parenting has been, each of our five children has been able to forgive when we confess our failings. No matter how far astray any of our children wanders, the road home is instantly traversed when they ask for forgiveness. As a result, our relationships with our kids have ripened into the deepest friendships of our lives.

Matthew 5:9

In the workplace and public arena we experience power politics, labor strife, racial and class conflict. Acrimony and accusation, strikes and lockouts, closed doors, and privileged circles mar our social well being and undermine our hopes for the future. Without reconciliation we will destroy each other. Jesus says, "Blessed are the peacemakers." A Christian peacemaker is someone who prays and works for reconciliation because he has been forgiven and reconciled to God. God promises answers to our prayer:

Jeremiah 29:7

Seek the peace and prosperity of the city to which I have carried you into exile. Pray to the Lord for it, because if it prospers, you too will prosper.

The practice of forgiveness can be applied to every relationship – no matter how deep the problem. Broken family relationships need healing. Marriages lie in scattered shards of unresolved hurt. Friends are separated by careless words. An office team loses friendship and chemistry. A church is reduced to gossip and accusation. Fill in your own blank. Nothing is beyond the reach of Jesus.

DAY 6

DAY 6

Prayerful Pondering

Questions for Reflection

Sin is an archery term that simply means to "miss the mark." Often we think of sin simply as the obvious external negative deeds we commit, such lying, cheating, or stealing.

Yet we must also be mindful to equally confess our "righteous deeds" – the things that we rely on to justify our own righteousness and goodness to stand before God. Compared to God's holiness, even our righteous deeds are filthy rags.

Taking it deeper, God also reveals our sin at a deeper level – to our thoughts, attitudes, and motives. Even doing an externally good act with a bad attitude or for an ill motive is sin that should be confessed at the cross.

* In light of God's holiness and glory as the standard, what areas of your life – thoughts, motives, words, actions – is God bringing to light for you to confess?

* How quickly are you able to resolve conflict and forgive others? Or how do you avoid conflict and act as a false peace keeper?

* Which situational or relational conflicts in the immediate world around you could use your prayers and peacemaking actions?

Summary of Key Idea(s)

What key thought(s) do you want to remember or revisit?

Prayer Prompts: *Use these points to guide your prayers. Try writing out your prayers.*

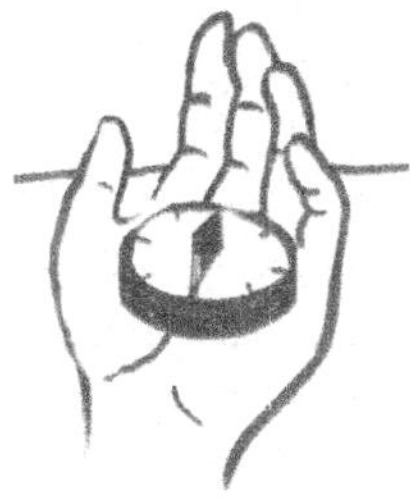

When we pray "Forgive us our sins as we forgive those who have sinned against us":

* We thank Jesus for the high price he paid to make forgiveness and reconciliation possible. We bring our hearts to Jesus, asking for courage and humility to acknowledge and confess our sin.
* We receive God's cleansing of our sin through Jesus' sacrifice and joyfully accept God's free and abundant grace. We bring our wounds to Jesus and his healing streams.
* As we are forgiven, and as we are healing, we find grace, courage, and power to forgive others who have sinned against us. We bring them to Jesus in prayer. We ask for God to open the door for the right opportunities for reconciliation.
* We pray to be peacemakers in the relationships and situations in the world around us.

DAY 6

Prayer Practice:
Preparing for a Daily Pattern for Prayer

Overview

Throughout this book, we will lead you through a pattern and sequence for prayer that focuses on one priority from Jesus' prayer each day. Today you will apply the pattern to "forgive us our sins as we forgive those who have sinned against us."

Pattern for Prayer ► *Applied to "Forgive us our sins"*

1 Priority & Promise

Praise God for his promises & priorities

Start by focusing on the priority **UPWARD to God.** Allow the Holy Spirit to guide you through the priority for the day.

Praise Jesus for the priority. Meditate on **what it means**, what it reveals about God, about Jesus' passion and purpose.

* *Thank God for his provision of Jesus' sacrifice to make forgiveness and reconciliation possible. Meditate on his abundant grace and mercy to forgive our sin and guilt.*

2 Passions

Pray God's promises & priorities into **your own heart**

Next pray the priority **INWARD into your heart.** Talk with God about your present heart state, allowing him to thoroughly examine and encourage you.

Ask Jesus to **transform your heart** and life to be more like his.

* *Are there any difficult relationships where you have been harbouring resentment, anger, or unforgiveness toward someone who has hurt you? Confess these to Christ.*
* *Receive the richness and joy of God's forgiveness. Thank him for freedom from sin and guilt.*

3 People

Pray God's promises as a **blessing to others**

Now pray **OUTWARD for others to experience more of God**'s promises.

Pray for **people,** your loved ones, other individuals, ministries, your church, city, and the world.

* *Is there a current context in your life – family, friends, work, community – where you are experiencing relational brokenness? Ask for God's perspective on the situation. Pray for forgiveness, reconciliation, and healing.*
* *Pray for the unity within your church body. Pray for the unity of the churches in your city.*

4 Praise

Praise God for all his blessings

End by **praising God** for his blessings and answers to prayer.

Recall how God has been present. Remember to **thank** him.

* *Praise God for his forgiving grace. Thank him for answers, blessings, or insights he reveals to you in your prayers.*

Personal Pattern for Prayer

Your prayer life will grow in depth, direction, passion and purpose by praying through one priority of Jesus' prayer each day using this sequence. Use Jesus' prayer as a framework to map your prayer. A further guide to this prayer pattern begins on page 107.

Personal Prayer Response

1 Priority & Promise

Praise God for his promises and priorities

2 Passions

Pray God's promises & priorities into your own heart

3 People

Pray God's promises as a blessing to others

4 Praise

Praise God for all his blessings

LEAD US

NOT INTO TEMPTATION BUT DELIVER US FROM EVIL

DAY 1 2 3 4 5 6 **7**

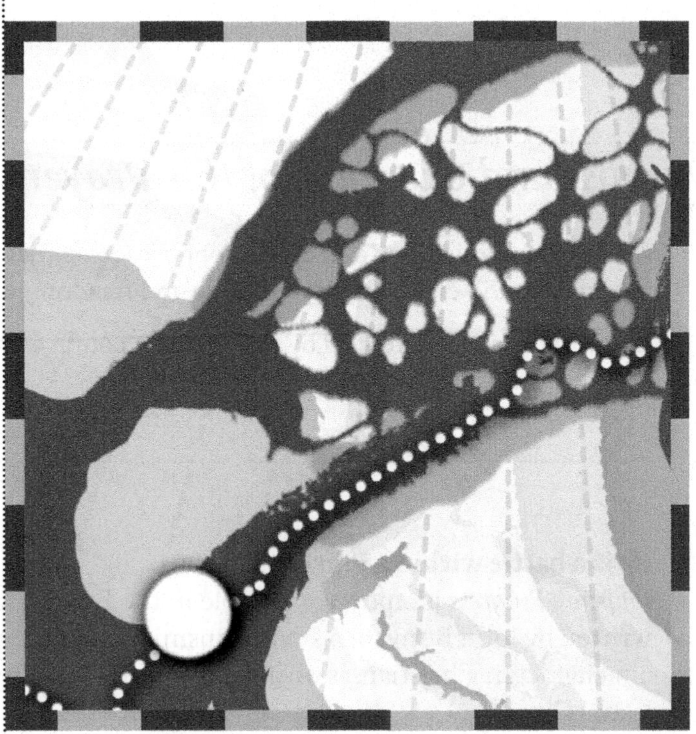

To have prayed well is to have fought well.
EDWARD MCKENDREE BOUNDS

The devil trembles when he sees God's weakest child on his knees.
ANONYMOUS

DAY 7

LEAD US NOT INTO TEMPTATION BUT DELIVER US FROM EVIL

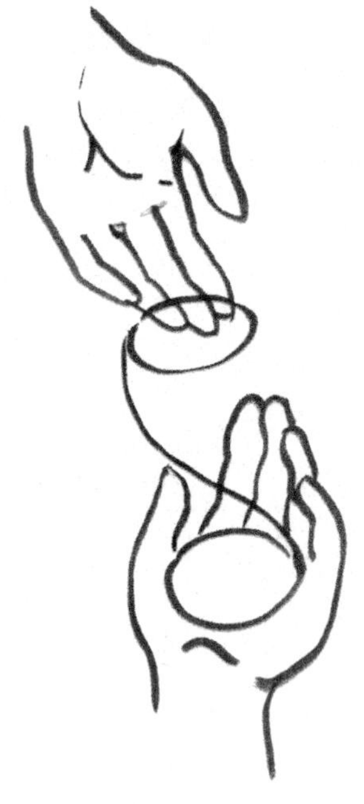

Today's Priority

* In this request we find courage and power to "defend the faith" and defend our personal faith. With open eyes of faith we work between two worlds – the visible and invisible.

Purpose and Outcome of this Prayer

* We advance against seen and unseen opposition so that men, women, and children will experience the healing and freedom Jesus gives.
* Our life will be characterized by Christ-given courage and power.

Life is a battle within a journey.

Pilgrim's Progress is a popular parable in the English language. It was written by John Bunyan, a simple tinsmith, while in prison for his faith. The main character, Christian, is on a journey from the City of Destruction to the Celestial City.

Prayer is violence. It consists in banging and slamming on the gates of heaven until they open. MARSHALL MCLUHAN

Christian's adventures read like a military campaign as well as a pilgrimage. His travel companions, Faithful and Hopeful, help to sustain him. He faces seen and unseen foes. He is tempted by characters like Slothful and Mr. Legality. Christian falls into the Slough of Despond, a place of depression. He spends time in Doubting Castle, relentlessly beaten by Giant Despair. He is tempted by sensual pleasure and ambition in the city of Vanity Fair. In the crucial battle, Christian goes head to head with Apollyon, (another name for Satan), who is the malevolent "ruler of this world":

> *Apollyon spread himself over the width of the road in front of Christian. "I have no fear," he growled. "Prepare to die. I swear by my infernal den you shall go no further." With that, flew a flaming dart at Christian's breast. The darts came thick and fast like a driving hailstorm....*

Christian defends himself with the shield of faith and the sword of truth. He is guarded by "All Prayer," the comprehensive defense and weapon of faith.

Bunyan's imagery is close to the Biblical language and metaphor. From the Bible's perspective, every person's life is a journey – with a beginning, middle, and end. In between there are trials and temptations, with victories won and battles lost. The Christian life is a war within a journey.

When we pray, "Lead us not into temptation, but deliver us from evil," we are asking for at least four things. First, we ask for God to lead us in his paths each and every day. Second, we pray for eyes of faith to see the whole of reality – what is seen and what is unseen. Third, we ask God to give us vigilance and to defend us from temptations and trials. Fourth, we ask for God's guiding presence and power so that his kingdom advances in and through his praying people.

1. In this journey we ask for God to lead us

When we pray, "lead us not into temptation," we are implicitly asking our heavenly father to be our guide and companion through the journey and battles of life until, safe at last, we come home to his heavenly kingdom. Our journey is not a solo quest for spiritual enlightenment or a heroic struggle of individual courage and resolve. We are guided and strengthened by God's Spirit each and every day.

God teaches the lesson of his leading to the Israelites as they journey for forty years through the wilderness. He goes before them in a pillar of cloud by day and a pillar of fire by night:

> *In all the travels of the Israelites, whenever the cloud lifted from above the tabernacle, they would set out; but if the cloud did not lift, they did not set out—until the day it lifted. So the cloud of the LORD was over the tabernacle by day, and fire was in the cloud by night, in the sight of all the house of Israel during all their travels.*

Exodus 40:36-38

The pillar is a picture or image of the Holy Spirit in the midst of the children of God and in the life of a believer. Being led by God's Spirit is a summary of the Christian journey:

> *Those who are led by the Spirit of God are sons of God.*

Romans 8:14

To be led means to follow. To follow Jesus is what it means to be a disciple. At the beginning of his ministry, he calls to his disciples, "Follow me!" At the end of his ministry he says again, "Follow me!" In between these two callings is a life of following Jesus. The same is true for every Christian.

John 1:43, 21:19

When we pray, "lead us not into temptation," we acknowledge that life's path is often hard and painful – filled with trials and temptations. The original word for "temptation" means both trial and testing. No one should ask for temptation. However, we know that our father in heaven permits it – for our good and for his holy and loving purposes. When we ask God to lead us, we are praying that God will give us grace to face, courage to endure, and power to overcome temptation. An old hymn spells out the continual guiding presence of God:

> *When through fiery trials thy pathway shall lie,*
> *My grace all-sufficient shall be thy supply.*

Jesus provides the perfect example of following his heavenly father when he faces temptation in the Garden of Gethsemane:

> *Going a little farther, he fell with his face to the ground and prayed, "My Father, if it is possible, may this cup be taken from me. Yet not as I will, but as you will."*

Matthew 26:39

Jesus is asking, if possible, to be led away from the last temptation – dying on a cross. At the same time he is praying for grace to accept God's leading and for courage to endure it. He knows that victory over all temptation, and over sin and death itself, will be the outcome of the cross.

We share our prayer with Jesus when we pray "Lead us not into temptation." We experience suffering and loss. We endure. Following him, we come through to victory.

2. To advance, we ask for eyes of faith to see the whole picture

Christians are accused of being narrow. This might be true in the case of some. However, from a metaphysical perspective, the Christian worldview is broader and deeper than the atheist or agnostic worldview. A Christian perceives physical and spiritual reality as a whole, the unseen as well as seen. Invisible and visible are interrelated and equally important dimensions to the universe.

This seen world is inseparably connected to the unseen:

Acts 17:28

In him we live and move and have our being.

The visible world derives its being from the invisible world:

Hebrews 11:3

By faith we understand that universe was formed at God's command,
so that what is seen is not made of what is visible.

What we see reveals the eternal reality behind it:

Romans 1:20

Since what may be known about God is plain to them, because God made it plain to them. For since the creation of the world God's invisible qualities – his eternal power and divine nature – have been clearly seen...so that men are without excuse.

Our universe is a temporary shadow of a greater eternal and unchanging reality:

2 Corinthians 4:18

So we fix our eyes on what is unseen. For what is seen is temporary,
but what is unseen is eternal.

When mathematician and philosopher, Bertrand Russell, was asked why he did not believe in a Creator he simply answered, "I have no need of that hypothesis." Considering the advance and accumulation of new discoveries in every branch of knowledge, we wonder how Russell could be so confident.

For example, Albert Einstein was perhaps the greatest genius of the twentieth century. When he devised the theories of special and general relativity, it was assumed that he discovered the key to understanding the universe. He linked space, time, and gravity with $e=mc^2$. However, we now realize this amazing discovery was only a part of a far greater picture.

As late as 1924 Einstein and everyone else thought that the Milky Way constituted the universe. Now we know that there are as many as 100 billion other galaxies in the universe – each with more than 100 billion stars! Einstein "saw" only a small part of the picture. Einstein believed the universe and its stars were static. Now we know that the universe is expanding and all the stars and galaxies are flying apart from each other at an ever accelerating rate, launched from a Big Bang.

Einstein believed that gravity and electro-magnetism were the main forces of the universe. Since then, scientists have discovered the strong and weak forces of the atom – the "small half" of the universe. We know these sub-atomic forces exist but how they operate is a mystery. Niels Bohr and Werner Heisenberg "proved" that we cannot directly measure motion and force in the sub-atomic realm.

Albert Einstein was right about so much. We understand our world in a fuller and better way because of him. Yet he was aware of the smallest fraction of what is. The more we learn, the more we are confronted by the unknowns of this universe. It is awesome and mysterious at its very core. Scientists speak about a multi-dimension universe, or parallel universes with increasing plausibility. Well known physicists, John Webb (New South Wales), and John Barrow (Cambridge) suggest:

> *The constants we observe [gravity, light, and mass of the electron] may not, in fact, be the truly fundamental ones. Those live in the higher-dimensional space and we see only their three-dimensional "shadows"...In the Grand Scheme of things, our observable universe is thought to be a small part of a multiverse...*
> ~Inconstant Constants, Scientific America *June 2005*

Such statements should produce openness in every thoughtful mind and heart. We should invite new discovery, welcome new paradigms, and not hold tightly to a safe and familiar picture. A close-minded inertia sets in when we fear ideas which might upset the applecart of our current worldview. When the atheist and materialist simply discount the possibility of God and an unseen spiritual reality, they are being closed minded and are missing the greater half of reality.

> *Pray or be prey – a prey to fears, to futilities, to ineffectiveness.*
> E. Stanley Jones

A brilliant friend, who for most of her life was agnostic, has recently begun to read the Bible. Her reasons are interesting. She was taking a graduate class in biology. Her teacher was a very vocal and adamant atheist. In fact he was so adamant that he ridiculed any religious question or observation. My friend was offended by his negative attitude, and started being a 'devil's advocate.' In the meantime she realized, in her own words, "there just has to be more than what we can see and measure," and so decided to find out for herself about God.

We can be excited about all we are learning but humble and open about what we do not know and may yet discover. We can continue to explore and enjoy the universe we see, but be open to a far greater reality of which this seen world is only a part.

Where does prayer fit in this? Prayer connects us to God who created and understands the entire universe, in all its visible and invisible realities. Prayer is like a spiritual Hubble telescope, lifting us far above the earth's perspective to see the entire cosmos like God sees it. As we pray, glimpses of invisible galaxies come into view.

This directly relates to our request, "Lead us not into temptation." Because God creates everything visible and invisible, these two "halves" are deeply related and in constant interplay. Seen and unseen are a complex interplay of physical forces and of good and evil personalities – including people, angels, and demons. These seen and unseen realms and those who occupy them are in constant relation. Forces of good and evil are in constant conflict.

This is the Christian worldview. A seen and unseen battle goes on each and every day. As spiritual and physical beings, each of us is poised in between:

> *Like the bacteria on the microscopic level, so these co-inhabiting pests on the macroscopic permeate our whole life invisibly and are the real explanation of that fatal bent which is the main lesson of history. ~CS Lewis,* Perelandra

Every person, community, church, and Christian is engaged in a very real battle against temptation, guilt, and despair. The instrument of attack can be other people, social forces, media, unseen personalities, or simply one's own unbelief and self-doubt. This fight matters. If we quit and give in there will be no victory. Yet ultimately – in the final hour – Jesus himself will physically appear with his angels and defeat all of his and our enemies.

1 Peter 5:8-11

> *Be self-controlled and alert. Your enemy the devil prowls around like a roaring lion looking for someone to devour. Resist him, standing firm in the faith, because you know that your brothers throughout the world are undergoing the same kind of sufferings.*
>
> *And the God of all grace, who called you to his eternal glory in Christ, after you have suffered a little while, will himself restore you and make you strong, firm, and steadfast. To him be the power for ever and ever. Amen.*

Prayer connects us to the power and presence of Jesus, our coming King. As we pray in expectation, his resurrection life flows into our hearts by the Holy Spirit he gives us. He enables us to defend against every seen and unseen enemy, and to advance in his promised victory.

3. We pray to withstand temptation

In this battle of the visible and invisible, we fight different varieties of temptation on different fronts. There are at least four battle lines where temptation occurs. First, Satan uses the weakness of our nature to tempt us. Second, temptation surrounds us – permeating our cities and world. Third, false teaching about Jesus and his purpose keeps people from God. Fourth, the chief target of trial and temptation is faith itself.

First of all, we are tempted through the weakness of our fallen nature. Nowhere is this stated more clearly than by the apostle John:

1John 2:15-17

> *Do not love the world or anything in the world. If anyone loves the world, the love of the Father is not in him. For everything in the world –* ***the cravings of sinful man, the lust of his eyes and the boasting of what he has and does*** *– comes not from the Father but from the world. The world and its desires pass away, but the man who does the will of God lives forever.*

Inordinate desire, deviant passion, envy and avarice, arrogance, hatred, and pride are within each of us. This inner corruption accounts for much of the bloodshed, brokenness, and betrayal found in the human story. Though he loves us, Jesus teaches the same truth without compromise:

Matthew 15:19

> *For out of the heart proceed evil thoughts, murders, adulteries, fornications, thefts, false witness, blasphemies.*

This "interior dislocation of the soul" (Dorothy Sayers) misdirects each one of us. Our own inner compulsion (not God or the devil) leads us into every temptation:

> *When tempted, no one should say, "God is tempting me." For God cannot be tempted by evil, nor does he tempt anyone; but each one is tempted when, by his own evil desire, he is dragged away and enticed. Then, after desire has conceived, it gives birth to sin; and sin, when it is full-grown, gives birth to death.*

James 1:13-15

Second, temptation surrounds us. As pollution clogs the air of the cities of the world, so we live in an atmosphere of temptation. Much of our world has turned from God. It is literally "ungodly." In our secular culture we edit God from the picture. We attempt to live life without his purpose, his power, or his presence.

This atmosphere of ungodliness envelopes us. It is contagious. I remember spending a good deal of time driving a car with a working colleague. He smoked as we drove. In just a few weeks, my former addiction to nicotine and constant craving for tobacco was renewed in full force just by hanging around with someone who smoked. In the same way, no matter how wonderful the creation and people can be, the atmosphere of this world is polluted with sin and temptation. We need the fresh air of God's grace and good news to clean the air. We need prayer to breathe the fresh air of heaven.

Through prayer we share the almightiness of God.
LUTHER

In all times and places there is abundant temptation. However today is different. The flow has increased from a stream to a river because of the incredible power of the media. Sexual exploitation and predation are fueled by "sexy" magazine covers, promiscuous sitcoms, salacious talk shows, and seductive advertising.

From the Internet flows rivers of good and rivers of evil - or a toxic mixture of both. Through the Internet greed, avarice, envy, lust, comparison, slander, and every other passion are excited in increasing frequency and intensity. Little is being done to slow the avalanche. We reserve moral outrage for those who would try to restrict our access to this "information." One person noted, "Even to avoid evil makes one a marked man." Though not a Christian, W.B. Yeats lamented about this modern age, "The best lack all conviction. The worst are filled with passionate intensity." We pray fervently to withstand temptation because we are constantly surrounded by it.

Third, moral and spiritual assault comes in the form of false teaching. For example, a popular and well written adventure novel, *The Da Vinci Code* represents Jesus as a pagan leader who participated in ritual sex and sired children through Mary Magdalene. Mary is the "Holy Grail" who received Christ and bore his children and she is deserving of our worship. Though none of the alleged documents Brown uses to support his argument have ever been discovered, he represents this lie as history. Because so few know the Bible's portrait of Jesus, enormous numbers are drawn in and are dead serious about his viewpoints. (*Breaking the Da Vinci Code* by Peter Jones is a good antidote).

The Bible warns that in every age, new "Christs" will arise. The objective of these "antichrists" is to mislead believers and to prevent others from getting to know who Jesus really is:

Matthew 24:4,5

> *Jesus answered: "Watch out that no one deceives you. For many will come in my name, claiming, 'I am the Christ,' and will deceive many."*

When we pray, "Lead us not into temptation," we pray for faith to resist false teachings about Christ.

Fourth, the trials, sufferings and betrayals of life tempt us to question or even abandon our faith in God. Jesus points out that we are easily tempted to doubt God. We are "men of little faith." It is really this doubting of God which is at the root of every temptation. If we are going to pray our way through temptation we will have to understand this. The primary assault of evil is against our faith.

Our spiritual life is like a ship. Faith is the hull. In naval warfare, if the hull is strong and holds, little significant damage results from a cannon attack. Only if the hull is weak, or the caliber of the cannon is sufficient, will there be penetration to the heart of the vessel. In *Master and Commander,* recall the first futile attempts of the British ship against the double thick hull of the French ship. Cannon balls simply bounced off.

In the same way, every assault of evil is first directed at this hull – our faith. The enemy's intent is to breach our connection to God. Using accusation, trial, and temptation, he wants us to take our eyes off of God and to question his goodness, power and love. If he succeeds – the hull is breached and we begin to sink.

Whenever we fall into sin, our faith falls first. Once we doubt the goodness, grace and power of God we are immediately vulnerable. On our own we are outgunned and outmanned by a superior enemy.

Luke 22:32

1 John 5:4

As we pray, Jesus strengthens and comforts us in temptation: "I have prayed that your faith might stand." Consider the trials and temptations of Job. Pummeled by the loss of his property, the death of his children, and the accusations of his "friends," Job is tempted to "curse God and die." However, Job is strengthened by God. "I know that my redeemer lives!" He endures. His faith stands. For all his weakness Job comes out the victor. "This is the victory – our faith."

While every believer sins every day in word, thought and deed, by Jesus' grace and power, his or her faith perseveres. The apostle Paul encourages us:

1 Corinthians 10:13

> *God will not permit you to be tempted beyond what you are able to endure but when you are tempted he will also provide a way out that you may be able to withstand it.*

Paul is not saying that we will never fall into sin. That is an impossibility. We are sinners and there is no sinless existence this side of heaven. What he means is that our reliance, trust, and loyalty to God will survive the trial. We will be tempted, we will sometimes fail, but by his grace and power we will grow in faith and live to fight another day.

As we ask God not to lead us into temptation our greatest encouragement is Jesus himself. He endured every temptation Satan could throw at him (see Luke 4:1-13). He met and conquered temptation in the garden and at the cross. One reason he did all this is so that he would be able to defend and protect us against every temptation we face:

Because he himself suffered when he was tempted,
he is able to help those who are being tempted.

Hebrews 2:18

4. We ask for God's guiding presence and power so that his kingdom advances

This prayer moves from defense, "Lead us not into temptation" to advance, "But deliver us from evil." In spiritual warfare we move from defense to advance. Ultimately we not only survive the battles of life, we win.

The reason for this is Jesus. His victory at the cross and empty tomb is decisive and complete. In the most important sense, Jesus has already conquered his enemies. Sin, death, and all evil personalities and powers are rendered powerless in the accomplishment of his finished work. The "wrap up" is soon coming.

The present age is a brief moment of history. It is like the end of World War II. The decisive battle was the allied victory at Normandy. After this battle it was only one year before complete surrender and the signing of treaties.

And having disarmed the powers and authorities, he made a public spectacle of them, triumphing over them by the cross.

Colossians 2:15

In prayer, by faith, a believer appropriates and participates in Jesus' victory in every spiritual and practical area of this life. There is no dualism between a practical and a spiritual victory. Jesus' victory is unseen and seen, in heaven and on earth:

The Spirit of the Lord is on me, because he has anointed me to preach good news to the poor. He has sent me to proclaim freedom for the prisoners and recovery of sight for the blind, to release the oppressed, to proclaim the year of the Lord's favor.

Luke 4:18

The victory we share with Jesus is seen and unseen, practical and spiritual. For example, we work with a local ministry for sexually exploited women and their children called *Genesis Vancouver*. When we pray for a sexually exploited woman to be delivered, we desire her to experience the grace of forgiveness and spiritual healing. We also ask for her to be delivered from the pimps, johns, and abusive people who prey on her and use her as a slave. Our prayers and our actions have this holistic intent. Anything less would be less than Jesus intends:

This is part of the prayer for the Kingdom: it is the prayer that the forces of destruction, of dehumanization, of anti-creation, of anti-redemption may be bound and gagged, and that God's good world may escape from being sucked down into their morass. ~NT Wright

During the great awakening in the eighteenth century, George Whitefield, Jonathan Edwards and the Wesley brothers led the way for a spiritual and practical revival. Going where there were no churches, they preached grace and practiced justice in the gin-alleys, coal towns, prisons, and asylums of their day.

As they were preaching, they brought blankets, food, and comfort to relieve the sufferings of these people. John Wesley said, "There is no Christianity that is not a social Christianity."

One hundred years later, their labors bore mature fruit. On the back seats of English parliament, William Wilberforce was overheard praying, "More light Lord! More light!" After years of political battle, only a few days before he died, slavery was abolished throughout the British Empire.

Jesus' kingdom includes heaven and earth. When we pray, "deliver us from evil," we include social justice and mercy:

Micah 6:8

What does the Lord require of you, O man,
But to do justice, and to love mercy and
To walk humbly with your God?

Prayer is the key to victory in all spiritual warfare. Karl Barth writes, "When God's people clasp their hands in prayer, it is the beginning of an uprising against the disorder of the world." When we pray, God promises he will act.

Psalm 12:5

"Because of the oppression of the weak
and the groaning of the needy,
I will now arise," says the LORD .
"I will protect them from those who malign them."

Psalm 72:12-14

For he will deliver the needy who cry out,
the afflicted who have no one to help.
He will take pity on the weak and the needy
and save the needy from death.
He will rescue them from oppression and violence,
for precious is their blood in his sight.

When we pray, Jesus will give us courage for each day's battle:

Ephesians 6:10-12,18

Finally, be strong in the Lord and in his mighty power. Put on the full armor of God so that you can take your stand against the devil's schemes. For our struggle is not against flesh and blood, but against the rulers, against the authorities, against the powers of this dark world and against the spiritual forces of evil in the heavenly realms... ***And pray in the Spirit on all occasions with all kinds of prayers and requests.*** *With this in mind, be alert and always keep on praying for all the saints.*

DAY 7

Prayerful Pondering

Questions for Reflection

* How have you experienced courage through prayer?

* What battles are you personally fighting where you need Jesus to deliver you – a habitual sin or temptation, a negative thought pattern, cultural pressures, despair through a trial? Can you picture what freedom in Christ's resurrection power looks like? Consider that Jesus is praying for you. How does this give you hope?

* Where in the world around you do you see conflict between light and dark forces? What injustices can you pray for?

Summary of Key Idea(s) *What key thought(s) do you want to remember or revisit?*

Prayer Prompts: *Use these points to guide your prayers. Try writing out your prayers.*

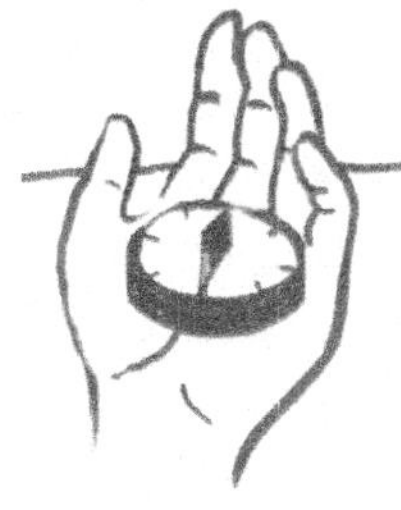

When we pray "Lead us not into temptation, but deliver us from evil":

* We pray for eyes of faith to see from God's perspective the trials in our own lives, and to see the realities of spiritual forces in conflict in the world around us.
* We recognize God's guidance and presence with us, and Christ's resurrection power, to resist temptation, and to endure and overcome trials.
* We ask God to defend us with spiritual protection, and advance us in his power.
* We pray for others who are entangled in difficulties or trials, and pray for Jesus to defend and deliver them.
* We pray for the restraint of evil forces in our city and world. We pray for God's goodness and power to prevail.

DAY 7

Prayer Practice:
Preparing for a Daily Pattern for Prayer

Overview

Throughout this book, we will lead you through a pattern and sequence for prayer that focuses on one priority from Jesus' prayer each day. Today you will apply the pattern to "Lead us not into temptation, but deliver us from evil."

Pattern for Prayer ► *Applied to "Lead us and deliver us"*

1 *Priority & Promise*

Praise God for his promises & priorities

Start by focusing on the priority **UPWARD to God.** Allow the Holy Spirit to guide you through the priority for the day.

Praise Jesus for the priority. Meditate on **what it means,** what it reveals about God, about Jesus' passion and purpose.

* *Ponder and thank God for all the spiritual blessings he has given you. Praise him for his resurrection power and ability to deliver you. Thank him for his guidance and presence throughout all your trials.*

2 *Passions*

Pray God's promises & priorities into **your own heart**

Next pray the priority **INWARD into your heart.** Talk with God about your present heart state, allowing him to thoroughly examine and encourage you.

Ask Jesus to **transform your heart** and life to be more like his.

* *Where do you see growing confidence and courage in Christ's power in your life? Thank him for it.*
* *Pray about an area in your life in which you need Christ to deliver you. Confess any unbelief, resignation to sin, or self-effort to overcome it yourself. Focus instead on what Christ has already done for you. Ask for courage and confidence in Christ to stand and advance.*

3 *People*

Pray God's promises as a **blessing to others**

Now pray **OUTWARD for others to experience more of God**'s promises.

Pray for **people,** your loved ones, other individuals, ministries, your church, city, and the world.

* *Pray for the spiritual guidance, protection, purity, and integrity of your church and other churches.*
* *Pray for God's resurrection power to be realized in people's lives, especially those who struggle with trials and temptations. Pray for Jesus to defend and deliver them.*
* *Pray for God's kingdom to advance in your city. Pray for goodness and light to prevail over evil and darkness in your city and world.*

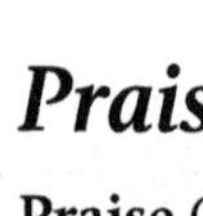

4 *Praise*

Praise God for all his blessings

End by **praising God** for his blessings and answers to prayer.

Recall how God has been present. Remember to **thank** him.

* *Praise God for his power and the victory we have in Jesus. Thank him for answers, blessings, or insights he reveals to you in your prayers.*

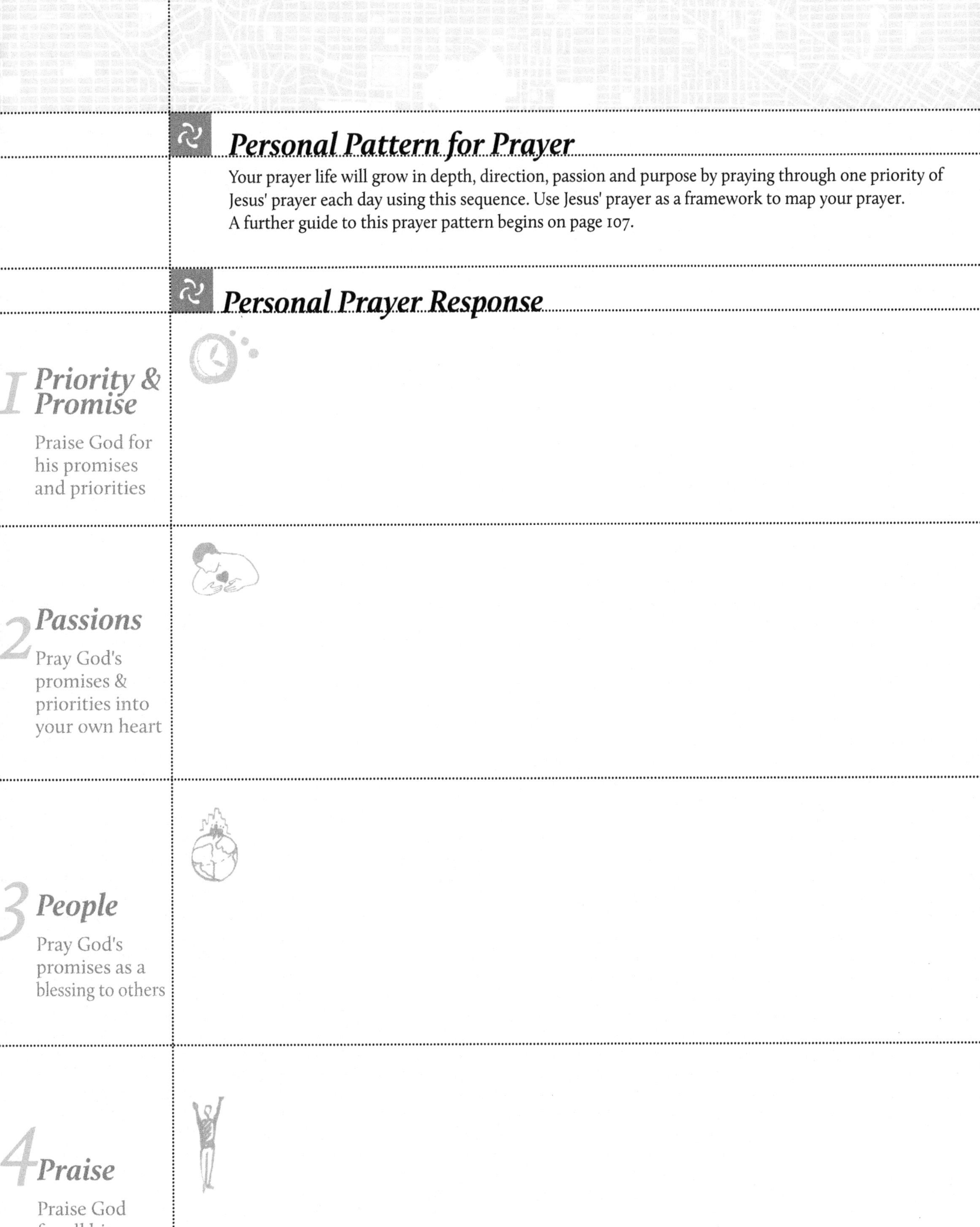

Personal Pattern for Prayer

Your prayer life will grow in depth, direction, passion and purpose by praying through one priority of Jesus' prayer each day using this sequence. Use Jesus' prayer as a framework to map your prayer.
A further guide to this prayer pattern begins on page 107.

Personal Prayer Response

1 Priority & Promise

Praise God for his promises and priorities

2 Passions

Pray God's promises & priorities into your own heart

3 People

Pray God's promises as a blessing to others

4 Praise

Praise God for all his blessings

Amen
Your Journey Ahead

DAY 1 2 3 4 5 6 7 ∞

Our Father *in heaven,*

***Holy** is your name*
*Your **kingdom come***
*Your **will be done** on earth*
as it is in heaven

*Give us this day our **daily bread***
***Forgive us** our debts*
*as we **forgive our debtors***

***Lead us** not into temptation*
*but **deliver us** from evil.*

This is Jesus' prayer. It is how he prayed as he lived and loved among us. It contains his agenda and his strategy for his present and coming kingdom. The key to growing in faith and reaching the world is found in its seven petitions. When God's children pray this prayer, the Father hears and answers. This is the prayer of his only Son. He always hears his Son. He will always hear the prayers of his adopted sons and daughters as they pray it too.

By giving us this prayer, Jesus is calling us to pray. He wants us to pray it faithfully. He invites us to pray it personally. He calls us to pray it as a community. A scene from *The Lord of the Rings* illustrates the call to prayer.

The beacons are the signal fires of Middle Earth. They are massive piles of dry timber, stacked in readiness, with a cauldron of oil suspended over the wood. A lit torch is always ready. A pair of sentries will light the beacon the instant they are called.

This signal fire kindles the memory of ancient allegiances – a united people against a common enemy. When under attack, the ancient city of Gondor will light its beacons, and all of Middle Earth will gather to defend her. It is a summons and signal for the return of the King. The lighting of the first beacon will start a chain reaction. Once the first beacon is lit, in minutes the other beacons of Middle Earth will burst into flame.

As the scene opens, the great city of Gondor is in trouble. Completely outnumbered, it is surrounded by legions of enemies. There are thousands of grotesque orcs, giant cave trolls, and mastodon-like oliphants with forty foot tusks and tree-trunk legs that juggernaut any army. This enemy is equipped with giant engines of war. Huge catapults hurl monstrous rocks. A massive cast-iron battering ram, filled with volcanic fire tears through the gates of the city. The Witch-King and his spirit-wraiths called "Nazgul" attack on dragons creating mayhem and spreading terror with their screams.

Behind this army is the hideous strength of Sauron – the evil spirit. His consuming intent and purpose is to destroy the race of men and to prevent the return of the King.

Within the city is another enemy. Denethor, the steward of Gondor is assigned to protect the city and prepare for the coming king. He refuses to do his part. His army is not ready. He clings to an empty title. He has studied the might and power of his enemy and his heart is filled with despair. "All hope is lost," he says. On first onslaught of the enemy he cries out, "Abandon your posts!" Worst of all, he refuses to light the beacons – to summon Middle Earth to war.

We see parallels in our present situation. We might value and enjoy our modern world, its great cities and advancements in technology and culture. Yet our cities and our churches have enemies – without and within. They are strong. The tide is advancing with increasing force. We appear seriously outgunned and outnumbered.

Secularism surrounds us. Relativism and hedonism break down the concept of truth and eat away at the foundations of right and wrong. There is no end of opponents attacking the simple truths of the gospel. A new and potent spirituality is growing in readiness and strength. It is not the spirituality of Jesus. It is a return to the spirits of paganism, otherwise known as "New Age."

Fueled by microchips and carried by laser filaments the engines of technology burn day and night 24/7. Television, radio, magazines, and the Internet bury us in advertising, shaping us into voracious consumers. Absorbed with accumulating, we become "One-Dimensional" (Herbert Marcus). The airwaves are filled with spectacle. Reality television, endless sporting events, and Jerry Springer or Geraldo voyeurism absorb our time and divert us from higher purposes. A frenzy of pornography and obscene chat lines clog the Internet. Relationships are reduced to sexual encounters.

This avalanche is increasing. It seems unstoppable. Technology advances without guidelines or brakes. Efforts to slow things down are brushed aside as idealism or phobia. Ethical and religious concerns are dismissed and ridiculed. Many have resigned the field in frustration or despair. Some have joined the other side.

Behind this assault against human dignity and conscience is an insidious, malevolent force. He is intent on crushing and eliminating any sense of eternal or transcendent purpose. His main target is the gospel of Jesus and the faith of his followers. Unsuspected and unseen, Satan is constantly working his plan.

In the meantime, within the city and within the church, like Denethor, the children of the King are strangely inactive. Some meet for an hour or two a week for consolation and fellowship. This "Sunday morning Christianity" does not make much of a difference. Christians are scattered in denomination and mega-church enclaves. A foreboding calm settles over church and city. There is fear in the air. Our enemy smells it. We have looked too long at the power and the intent of the enemy.

Yet there is a faithful remnant who knows what needs to be done. Jesus is calling us. His prayer is a summons – "Light the beacons of prayer!"

When we pray Jesus' prayer we make a great discovery. Praying it we recover our identity as children of the king. Within its petitions is a strategy for reaching and rescuing our communities and our cities. At its heart, this prayer is a yearning for the return of the King to rescue and deliver all those who wait for him.

The difference prayer makes

In the battle for Middle Earth, the tide turns when the beacons are lit. Gandalf tells Pippin to ignore Denethor. Out of view, Pippin scales the high tower to light the beacon. He gets to the top of the stack of dry timber. He spills the vat of oil on the wood. He grabs the torch and touches the wood. It bursts into flame – so explosively, it nearly ignites Pippin!

Next, we are carried in a zooming panorama across the mountain valley. Every thirty or forty miles, on the tops of the highest mountains, stands another beacon in clear sight of the previous. Other sentries, timber, oil, and torch, are waiting and ready. Seeing the fire at Gondor, one beacon after another explodes in flame. In a matter of minutes every beacon in Middle Earth is lit. As if the flames were leaping from one station to another, the land is lit with hope. A world changing process is set in motion. All the tribes and people of men are summoned to Gondor. Recalling their ancient allegiance, armies begin to muster to defend the city. The tide turns.

The long awaited king, Aragorn, sees the flaming beacons and prepares his battle plan and his return. It is time for him to assert his rightful rule and reign over middle earth. It is time to rescue the innocent. It is time to vanquish the enemy.

A similar scenario occurs when God's people set themselves to pray. To pray is to light the beacons. To pray Jesus' prayer is to summon the people of God to a united warfare of love and truth. It is a mighty cry for our king to lead us in battle.

Like flaming beacons, the fire of prayer is contagious. When even a handful offer up Spirit-filled prayers the process is set in motion. Nothing encourages God's children more than to hear the purpose-filled prayer of Jesus. As this prayer begins to burn, the hearts of others will burn too.

As we pray, momentum turns. We remember our ancient unity. We face our common foe. We unite to defend each other and to defend our neighbor and our cities. Hope replaces despair. Readiness to act replaces apathy. Our hearts are filled with love and compassion for others, rather than fear or envy. We discover the awesome power of the gospel to save and to heal. We experience the might of grace to overcome hatred and violence.

The present and coming king himself will visit us.

At the critical moment, Aragorn the rightful king, returns to the city. He comes in awesome power and with numberless unseen hosts. He and his spirit-army are unstoppable. The armies of Sauron have no defense against such an opponent. In a matter of minutes the city is regained, the besieged are rescued, and every foe is leveled to the ground.

Jesus is the present and coming king. When he comes no enemy can withstand his coming. He storms the gates of the city in answer to prayer. In unstoppable grace and power, he saves, heals, and rescues all who rely on him. He renews his church, transforms communities, rebuilds cities, and makes our streets safe to dwell in.

The seven purposes of Jesus will come to light as we pray his prayer.

He gives us hearts that cry out "Abba. Father!"

He reveals to us and refines us by his holiness.

His kingdom will come. Men, women, and children will be saved.

His will shall be done in the streets of the city – with wisdom, love and courage.

Simplicity and generosity will characterize us as his children. We will enjoy daily bread with thanksgiving.

Bitter feuds will be resolved as we learn to receive and extend forgiveness.

We will move from defending against temptations to advancing in spiritual battles.

He will hear and answer as we pray.

If my people who are called by my name, will humble themselves and pray –
I will turn and heal their land.

2 Chronicles 7:14

Come Jesus Come!

Prayerful Pondering

Questions for Reflection

* How have you seen God work through prayer during the course of this study?

* How will you light your beacon?

* Imagine: how would your life look if you began to consistently pray through the priorities of the Lord's prayer?

* What are a few practical ways you can integrate the Lord's prayer into *your personal life*? How about ways to incorporate it into *your corporate life* with others?

Summary of Key Idea(s) *What key thought(s) do you want to remember or revisit?*

Mapping your life through prayer

Crafting a Prayer Grid for Life

Overview

Throughout this book we have been praying through an upward-inward-outward sequence of prayer through the lens of each priority of Jesus' prayer:

1. **Priority & Promise:** *Praising God* for his priorities and promises (upward)
2. **Passions:** Praying God's priorities and promises *into your own heart* (inward)
3. **People:** Praying God's priorities and promises *into other people's lives* (outward)
4. **Praise:** *Praising God* for all his blessings and answers to prayer (upward)

By putting all the priorities together with this sequence in one place, you can create a prayer grid that serves as a map to guide your prayer life and note how Jesus' priorities express themselves in your life. (See sample on page 108.)

Purpose and Outcome of a Prayer Grid

You *are* what you pray: A good prayer grid will reflect who you are, and the calling, priorities, and passions God has shaped in you.

You *become* what you pray: An even better prayer grid will reflect who God wants you to become and will include His priorities uniquely expressed in your life. As you meet with God in prayer, He will transform you and motivate you to Kingdom vision and purpose.

A good prayer grid will be **in process**, just as you are in process. It will be **organic, growing, and connected to your life.** Like a carpenter's tool, your prayer grid should be **sharpened continually** to be useful. Your list will need to be adjusted as you change and as your heart is transformed through prayer, as your passions and calling become clearer, and as people, needs, and circumstances in your life change.

Why use a prayer grid?

* A prayer grid that uses the Lord's prayer as a framework **provides direction and purpose** to your prayer life. It helps you see how the people, places, and requests you are praying for fit into the bigger picture of God's plan. The priorities of Jesus' prayer are deep and vast enough to pray through until he comes again!

* Integrating a prayer grid into your broader prayer life is an encouraging way to **request, record, and recognize God's movement** in your life and world.

* A prayer grid guides your prayer life according to the Lord's Prayer as a **structured framework.** Following this structured guide gives you a place to return, like stepping back into a fitness routine or a Bible reading plan after a break or change in season.

* A prayer grid helps you to **prioritize and manage the volume** of prayer needs to bless others and your city in prayer.

appendix B | Building a Prayer Grid

PATTERN	Day 1	Day 2	Day 3	Day 4	Day 5	Day 6	Day 7
PRIORITY & PROMISE	Our **Father** in heaven	Our Father, **Holy** is your name	Our Father, **Your kingdom** come	Our Father, **Your will** be done	Our Father, Give us this day our **daily bread**	Our Father, **Forgive us** as we forgive our debtors	Our Father, **Lead us** not into temptation, deliver us
	Relationship & Prayer	Worship	Evangelism City renewal	Mercy Social justice	Contentment Generosity Simplicity	Unity Reconciliation	Guidance Advance
Pray God's **PASSIONS** into my own heart	release guilt embrace joy	see how my sins hurt God's heart	compassion boldness patience	obedience empathy to relate with others different than me	gratitude release greed	willingness to let go of my grudges	wisdom & strength to make wise choices
Pray God's blessing for other **PEOPLE**	friend who just became a Christian people in church to know God better	worship team community art show	conversations w/ co-workers opportunity to meet my neighbours family mission trip in our own city	friend's depression my sponsor child ministry to sexually exploited women	budgeting volunteer fundraising drive government leaders	church leaders bible study groups family conflict & healing	resist my temptations spiritual protection for church
PRESSING urgent requests				friend's struggle with cancer	unemployed friend to find a job	friend's divorce	friend's struggle w/ addiction
PRAISE for who he is & answers to my prayers	new sense of joy		going out with co-workers for lunch now		friend found work!		

* sample prayer items in a grid

Priority & Promise

Praise God for his promises and priorities

* Arrange your prayer life according to the Lord's prayer so that what you are praying for is balanced and aligned with Jesus' priorities. Pray through one priority each day. Start your prayer by meditating on the priority for the day – the priority becomes the lens through which you see and pray for the needs listed in your life and the world around you that day.
  * Our **Father** in heaven...Relationship & Prayer
  * **Holy** is your name ....Worship
  * Your **kingdom come** ....Evangelism & City Renewal
  * Your **will be done** on earth as in heaven..............Mercy & Social Justice
  * Give us this day our **daily bread**............................Generosity & Contentment
  * **Forgive us** as we forgive others ....Unity & Reconciliation
  * **Lead us** not into temptation but deliver us..........Guidance & Advance

Passions

Pray God's priorities into *your own heart*

* Then move to a time of praying for yourself – specifically praying God's priorities into your own heart and life. Focus on the priority of the day from above.
* This is the time in your prayer to allow God to thoroughly examine and encourage your heart affections according to his priorities and the values of his kingdom.
* Do not rush this part of the prayer sequence. This is key to keeping this tool free from legalism. This is what helps direct your prayer time in true hearing and relating to God.
* Ask for transformation and alignment of your heart to His heart and to the priorities that are His.

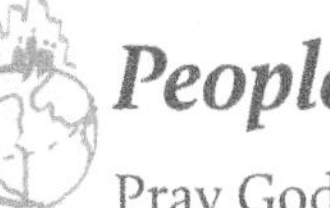

People

Pray God's promises as a *blessing to others*

* Pray for friends, individuals, missionaries, churches, ministries, organizations, people groups, etc. related to the priorities (if possible).
* Include all others wherever is most appropriate. Obviously people don't fit in a box.
* ***Pressing (Urgent) Needs***
  * Pray for urgent needs in your life, and for those around you, including church needs, and other "neighbours" in your life, and world crises.

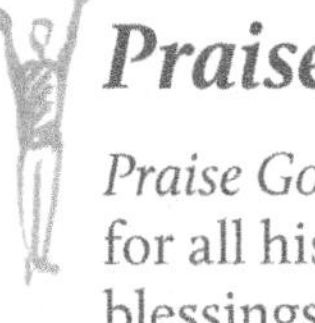

Praise

Praise God for all his blessings

* Periodically and regularly go through what you've been praying for through your list; record answers and praise God for them. Recognizing answers to your prayers builds faith and momentum to continue in prayer for greater things and makes you thirsty for more.

Blank Prayer Grid Template

Reminder Row*							
Pattern for request	Our Father in heaven	*Our Father,* Holy is your name	*Our Father,* Your kingdom come	*Our Father,* Your will be done on earth as it is in heaven	*Our Father,* Give us this day our daily bread	*Our Father,* Forgive us our debts as we forgive our debtors	*Our Father,* Lead us not into temptation, deliver us from evil
Priority of prayer	Sonship	Worship	Evangelism City Renewal	Mercy Social Justice	Generosity Contentment	Unity Reconciliation	Guidance Advance
Prayers for **Passions** of my heart (heart affections)							
Prayers for other **People**							
Praise for answers to my prayers							

* *After praying through a specific priority each day, make a check mark at the top of the column in the reminder row to help you track your prayer balance.*

Reminder Row*							
Pattern for request	Our Father in heaven	*Our Father,* Holy is your name	*Our Father,* Your kingdom come	*Our Father,* Your will be done on earth as it is in heaven	*Our Father,* Give us this day our daily bread	*Our Father,* Forgive us our debts as we forgive our debtors	*Our Father,* Lead us not into temptation, deliver us from evil
Priority of prayer	Sonship	Worship	Evangelism City Renewal	Mercy Social Justice	Generosity Contentment	Unity Reconciliation	Guidance Advance
Prayers for **Passions** of my heart (heart affections)							
Prayers for other **People**							
Praise for answers to my prayers							

* *After praying through a specific priority each day, make a check mark at the top of the column in the reminder row to help you track your prayer balance.*

appendix D

Prayer Grid Pointers

Like forming any new habit, praying through a prayer grid requires some adjustment at first. Here are a few notes to help you in the process.

First, creating and updating your grid is a helpful evaluative exercise to provide a snapshot of the health and balance of the priorities of your prayer life.

Second, praying through the prayer grid must be integrated into the unique rhythm of your life. Think of different ways you can incoporate it into your current routines – perhaps after your regular time in the Word, or during your shower, or as part of your daily commute, or during your gym workout or daily walk.

Be encouraged; it is not unusual to encounter resistance in forming a new habit, especially one with deep spiritual impact such as this one.

Persevere! Millions pray the Lord's prayer. Many have found this grid helpful in sustaining regular prayer. Keep picking your grid up again as you develop the habit of using it. Think of this tool as an organic guideline to which you can return after a break or lapse, like returing to a fitness routine or Bible reading plan.

"Preach the gospel to yourself" as you develop this new habit. God does not desire for us to offer him a works-righteousness form of prayer or earn his approval or attention by "saying enough prayers" or religiously using tools like this grid. These are simply tools to serve us; beware the temptation of becoming a slave to serving the tools or defining your prayer strength by frequency of praying through this grid. This tool is meant to feed into, supplement and direct your prayer life in accordance with Jesus' priorities.

Now for some practical ideas and reminders:

* **Don't fly over the "Passions of my heart affections" too quickly.** This is the part of your prayer time that is designed to help you draw near in relating to your heavenly Father's heart. This is key to to the list not becoming a legalistic ritual - it is what turns it into the experience of encountering your Father-God.

* **Common question: Is this prayer list only a list of praying for needs?** No, there should be all kinds of prayer interspersed throughout - praise, thanksgiving, confession, and listening prayer are naturally woven throughout your prayer. For example, praying "forgive us as we forgive others": *"Father, I praise you, for you are the one who ultimately forgives us and brings true reconciliation and unity with you first, that we can then extend it to others around us. You know I am currently working through a conflict. I confess and ask for forgiveness of my heart toward my friend. Despite the pain of working through the conflict, I thank you for the situation of this conflict, because it shows me an area I need to trust you to change in my heart. I ask that you would give me wisdom and humility to resolve it. I pray when that conversation comes, we will both see your light and hope in the situation..."*

* **Use the list as a trigger and reminder to pray for various requests.** Allow the Holy Spirit to lead you in specific prayers for people, places, and ministries.

* **Pray through one column/one priority a day at a time.** The priority of the day becomes the lens through which you see and pray for the needs in your list and in the world around you that day.

* **Use a "Reminder Row"** at the top of each column instead of days of the week. After praying each day, make a check mark at the top of the column to help you track your prayer balance. This allows flexibility to pray for the priority you are burdened for on any given day.

appendix E

Leading a Small Group Study

Here are a few suggestions and tips if you are preparing to lead a small group using this material as the focus of your study.

The study works best when group members read a chapter ahead of time and come prepared to discuss and pray in response to the material that week. Encourage participants (in preparation on their own) to summarize the chapter in their own words and consider the personal reflection questions at the end of each chapter.

For the weekly small group gathering, **plan for two foundational and equally important components** for each session you lead: A. discussion, and B. prayer.

A. **Group discussion.** Create/choose two or three key questions appropriate for group discussion of each chapter. Questions should aim for a two-fold purpose:

1. to flesh out understanding of key concepts; and
2. to begin to apply the principles into their own lives and the life of the church and city.

B. **Group prayer practice.**

To truly grow in the practice of prayer, you should plan to aim for equal time in discussion and equal time in prayer. Make it a priority to avoid "all talk and no prayer action" with all discussion and no actual praying. Rather, prayer allows us to see God in His full power which fills and moves us to action. We have found a few simple guidelines helpful in facilitating group prayer:

1. **Establish parameters for group prayer:**

Respect the ABCs of prayer:

* **Audible:** is a simple reminder that clear and audible prayers help others to pray in concerted spirit with the person praying out loud.
* **Brief:** Keep the ball rolling with short "popcorn prayers." Praying brief prayers, but as often as you like (compared to praying several items in one long list) keeps the dynamic moving along and helps people engage in group prayer.
* **Christ-centred:** Remind people that we are praying to "an audience of one" so that would mean no preaching or advice-giving to others in prayer, for example.

2. **Give clear direction on the focus of prayer.** Some suggestions:

* Use the Prayer Prompts at the end of each chapter to guide prayers.
* Pray through the sequence of the Prayer Practice Pattern (Priority, Passions, People, Praise) at the end of each chapter.
* Use specific Scripture related to each petition.
* If you are listing requests specific to your group, church, community, or city that are related to the chapter's petition, writing them on a whiteboard or having them available on a handout may help people to remember and keep track of the petitions.

3. **Plan for and pray with variety.**
Keep the ball rolling. Intersperse discussion and prayer, instead of leaving all the prayer until the end, where it will often drag on, or worse, get squeezed out completely from lengthy discussions. Alternate prayer times with people in various configurations.

For example, one session may start with a few minutes of discussion, then the whole group may respond with short sentence "arrow" prayers of praise. That may be followed by a few more minutes of discussion and brief highlights of specific prayer needs related to the city and church.

Then in groups of three or four, people may follow in praying specific petitions. Then may come a time for sharing answers to prayer or personal prayer requests, which may end with people praying in pairs for each other by name.

Just keep things moving. We have found the momentum to be slow and difficult when the whole group is left with extended periods of time for open, unguided prayer, or when one person dominates with a long drawn out prayer covering all the requests listed.

4. **Finally, and most important, prayer prepare!**

As you prepare for each session, soak your preparation in prayer. Pray for each member in your group. Pray for a Spirit of grace and supplication and God to be clearly present and guiding in your discussion and rich prayer times with your group. Ask for the Spirit to fill you with discernment to best lead your group in following the Spirit's movement.

Lead people to MEET JESUS IN PRAYER

ORDER PRAYER CURRENT RESOURCES www.prayercurrent.com

Please send orders to:
106 – 1033 Haro Street
Vancouver, BC V6E 1C8
CANADA. Ph: 778-383-1011
E: info@prayercurrent.com

PRAYER EVANGELISM: Introduce SEEKERS to Jesus

GOD IN THE CONVERSATION

Listen in on 12 inspiring conversations with diverse spiritual seekers that show **how conversation and prayer can bridge seekers to Jesus.** Excellent as a book club outreach.

JOURNEY IN PRAYER: Learning to pray with Jesus

Let Jesus' words in the Lord's prayer **share the gospel clearly** with seekers. Personal **journal pages** with prompts lead seekers to respond in prayer. Excellent as a **follow up to Alpha.**

PRAYER DISCIPLESHIP: Train CHRISTIANS in prayer

7 DAYS OF PRAYER with Jesus Small Group Study

Increase depth and breadth of your prayers through this 7 week study of **the Lord's prayer as a powerful pattern** for our lives and world. Learn a practical prayer grid as a **tool for personal daily prayer.** *Available in English, Chinese, and Spanish.*

PRAYER FOR THE CITY (+DVD) Bootcamp for Urban Mission

Train your leaders to **lead from the knees**, with tools to then **build God's people as a house of prayer** for all nations. This 12 lesson study is packed with **biblical foundations and practical tools for personal, corporate, and missional prayer.**

PRAYER LEADERSHIP: Train LEADERS to lead Prayer

Leading Dynamic Prayer

Empower pastors, church planters, missionaries, ministry leaders, and campus ministers to **intentionally disciple people** in kingdom prayer. Explore holistic, creative, practical ways of how to **bring dynamic prayer into any context.** An essential leader's guide to increase the effectiveness of all Prayer Current resources.

Title / Subtotal	Quantity	Unit Price	
God in the Conversation		$15	
Journey in Prayer		$10	
7 Days of Prayer with Jesus		$15	
Prayer for the City		$30	
Leading Dynamic Prayer		$20	
		Subtotal	
Less Discount *(5% on 10+, 15% on 50+ , 20% on 100+)*			

PLEASE FILL IN

OFFICE USE ONLY

PRINT CLEARLY: Name:________ Organization:________
Address:________ City:________
Prov/State:________ Post Code/ZIP ________ Phone:________
E-mail:________ Would you like to receive e-news? ☐ Yes
Payment: ☐ Cheque ☐ Visa ☐ Mastercard Card #________
Name on Card________ Expiry________
Signature________

Prayer Current helps people navigate life through prayer. Whether someone is just entering the waters or is an experienced traveler, Prayer Current provides inspiration and practical tools to grow in prayer, and to "pray it forward" by helping grow others in prayer.

Designed for life in the city and for personal or church use, Prayer Current resources engage people in a balance of reflection, interaction, study, actual prayer practice, and mission.

www.prayercurrent.com

CPSIA information can be obtained
at www.ICGtesting.com
Printed in the USA
LVOW03s0054221216
518194LV00003B/5/P

9 780986 663154